DAYS OF

ANGUISH,

DAYS OF HOPE

Bill Keith

DAYS OF ANGUISH, DAYS OF HOPE

Introduction by
ROBERT PRESTON TAYLOR
Chaplain, Major General, USAF

"Books for the Journey"
StoneGate Publishing Co., Inc.
Longview 2011

Library of Congress Catalog Card Number
76-6033

Printed in the United States of America

Seventh Edition

Copyright © 2011 by Bill Keith

StoneGate Publishing Co., Inc.
P. O. Box 8321
Longview, TX 75607
Stonegatebooks@aol.com

THE MILITARY CHAPLAINS ASSOCIATION HONORS AUTHOR

In 2009, the Military Chaplains Association – which has 900,000 members -- honored Bill Keith during the annual meeting in Fort Worth, Texas. The group presented him with a plaque that said:

"The Military Chaplains Association takes great pleasure in granting honorary life membership to Bill Keith."

Keith granted permission to MCA to print 5,000 copies of the book to be given to all active military chaplains and to the members of Congress.

To Mrs. Robert Preston Taylor, the faithful wife of General Taylor, who stood by his side through his long years of military service.

FOREWORD

During the writing of Days of Anguish, Days of Hope, two questions kept recurring in my research. First: Why, during World War II, did the Japanese treat their prisoners, and even their own men, so cruelly? Second: What really took place on the "hell ships," or the Japanese prisoners-of-war transports, about which so little has been written?

To answer the riddle of the cruel treatment of the POWs, I studied Japanese psychology and probed into the Japanese mind. This I did during the six years I lived in Japan. It soon became apparent that I would have to learn both spoken and written Japanese. During that very unique experience, I developed a basic understanding of the complicated Japanese mind and its implications for prisoners in their camps.

But I discovered that information about the hell ships was nonexistent. I visited the Philippines twice and interviewed government officials, former Filipino soldiers, and even older people on the streets who might remember something about the hell ships. Then I studied at the National Library in Manila and spent long hours in the "morgue" of the Manila Times.

With this background I began to piece together the story of combat chaplain Robert Preston Taylor's survival of the war in the Philippines, Bataan, the death march, the prison camps, and, of course, the hell ships.

Although Taylor himself was a major source of information – he gave me access to his personal diary of the war years, papers, etc. – information on his war years was still missing. So I returned to the Philippines and retraced the dreadful Bataan death march route, much of it on foot.

Bit by bit the story began to fit together and some of the long-awaited answers began to appear.

The combat chaplain's battles were not fought with demolition or cannon – but with biblical ideals implanted in men's hearts. These ideals were key factors in the survival of hundreds of the prisoners.

For instance, during the soldiers imprisonment in Cabanatuan Prison Camp, conditions were so bad it appeared the camp would be completely destroyed by starvation, disease and mistreatment. And, of course, the circumstances were basically the same on the infamous journeys of the hell ships.

Then an amazing thing took place as a genuine spiritual renewal swept through the camp. Chaplain Taylor was one of the leaders in that experience.

I originally allotted eight months to prepare this manuscript. It took four years. During that time, General Taylor has become one of my closest and dearest friends, and one of my personal heroes.

During the writing he kept reminding me: "Billy, we don't want to be bitter toward the Japanese. It was a great tragedy for that nation to undergo such trauma, just as it was for the prisoners of war in their camps. I learned to forgive them a long time ago."

Bill Keith

Contents

FOREWORD
INTRODUCTION
PROLOGUE

INTRODUCTION

Many years ago the Department of Defense provided a place for chaplains among men in uniform. During World War II, more than ten thousand chaplains served army, navy, and air corps personnel. At least one chaplain sailed with every thousand troops who departed for Africa, Europe, and the Far East.

Days of Anguish, Days of Hope retells the story of the combat chaplain and hosts of fighting men who lived and died in Japanese prison camps and on the ships at sea. This story is not imaginary – it is born out of experience and reality.

After thirty years, it is difficult to reconstruct the events exactly as they occurred. However, in this book we have an amazing likeness of the story, the way it actually happened.

Some of the greatest men in the world gave their lives for their country in the Philippines. They were devoted Americans, and many were faithful Christians. They loved their country and wanted to return to it and to the families they had left behind. Far too few ever realized that dream.

Those men were the real heroes of Bataan, the death march, the prison camps and the hell ships. Most of their names are long since forgotten. But what they did for the cause of freedom will live forever.

It is my hope that through the experience of this book we will all rededicate ourselves to freedom for all mankind and to our Lord who has proven Himself faithful in every circumstance.

Robert Preston Taylor

PROLOGUE

On August 16, 1962, President John F. Kennedy named Brigadier General Robert Preston Taylor Air Force Chief of Chaplains and promoted him to major general.

Taylor was summoned to the Pentagon, where he was handed the reins of leadership of all Air Force clergy.

The brilliance of that remarkable moment was the culmination of the twenty-two-year military journey of Robert Preston Taylor.

That tragic yet magnificent military journey led him through the torturous Bataan Death March and three-and-one-half years imprisonment in Japanese prisoner of war camps in the Philippines, Japan and Manchuria.

Days of Anguish, Days of Hope is the story of that imprisonment and Taylor's miraculous survival.

1.

ASSIGNMENT PHILIPPINES

On a Thursday morning in May 1941, the troop ship USAT Washington sailed into Manila Bay, the Philippines.

After waiting for more than an hour for clearance from port authorities, the Washington docked to Pier Seven, reported to be the longest in the world.

Clamor and excitement ringed the pier as the three thousand officers and young enlisted men disembarked from the ship that had brought them from San Francisco to the Far East command.

The blaring military band and cheering crowds that greeted the support troops and replacements temporarily masked the imminent threat of war.

It had already been a perfect day, Preston Taylor reflected, as he picked up his gear and prepared to leave the ship. And now Manila – beautiful Manila – the magnificent city extending out into the bay and beyond to the sloping hills.

Taylor, a lieutenant in the Army Air Corps – lean, rangy and the picture of discipline – that morning had been named regimental chaplain to the famous Thirty-first Infantry, an outfit with a proud military history. He had been told it was the only full American regiment in the Philippines and included a detachment of elite Philippine Scouts. They were quartered in the heart of Manila, the Cuartel de Espana, within the historic walled city. "Preston Taylor!" a familiar voice called to him as he stepped down the gangplank. "Welcome to the Philippines."

It was Chaplain Morris Day, a former classmate at Southwestern Seminary in Fort Worth, Texas, and he looked very happy until Taylor inquired about his family.

"Oh, they returned to the States last week," Day answered forlornly. "All dependents are being pulled out."

Colonel Alfred Oliver, chief of chaplains in the Philippines, and three other chaplains who had arrived on the Washington with Taylor, waited at the gate to Pier Seven. Colonel Oliver had said that orientation for the new chaplains would begin with a jaunt around Manila, so Taylor stepped into the ancient army bus and sat down beside Art Cleveland, a chaplain from the Christian Church.

Oliver instructed the driver to proceed down Dewey Boulevard.

"This street was named for Admiral George Dewey, the hero of the Philippines," the colonel began. "When war broke out between America and Spain, he was commander of the Asiatic squadron that destroyed the Spanish fleet. Pretty good show for the Navy."

The hull of a Spanish ship could still be seen anchored in the sand, a mute testimony to the war of 1898.

"Yes, sir, only six ships, too. Blew the Spanish fleet right of the water," Oliver added.

Walled gardens along the waterfront were aflame with rose-purple rhododendrons and large, showy China roses. Orchids, interspersed between the other flowers and green shrubs, created a panorama of color and symmetry.

The young men shot volley after volley of questions at Colonel Oliver. He was an old hand in the Orient, and had been in the chaplaincy fourteen years. The bus turned off Dewey Boulevard and headed toward the center of the city.

A triad of cultures – European, American and Oriental – decorated the Manila skyline. Church spires and belfries – symbols of Christianity – stood beside the Spanish and Eastern structures in the Asiatic capital.

The city became a living map Taylor had seen many times, but it was dotted with fifteenth-century houses and red rose bushes.

"That's Santo Domingo Cathedral," Oliver pointed out. "Each day its bells can be heard all throughout the city."

Downtown Manila was alive with thousands of people and the heavy traffic came to a standstill. Karamanta ponies, pulling two-wheeled carts down red cobblestone streets, sounded to Taylor like a sheriff's posse during a Fourth of July parade in Texas. Students milled around decorative fountains with figures and other ornaments of lead, bronze, stone and marble.

"Those little horses! Look at them, Preston!" Art Cleveland said.

"Their lifetime is very, very short," Colonel Oliver interrupted. "Their owners trot them to death.

The bus stopped at Santiago, the Royal Fortress. The colonel led them past the guards and into the compound. Once the fortress of Rajah Saliman, the last of the Philippine defenders of Maymilad, it was now General Headquarters for the United States Army, Philippine Command and General Douglas MacArthur's office was in the main building. A meticulously crafted replica of Jose Rizal stood outside.

"Governor Santiago de Ferva, for whom the fort is named, commissioned Antonio Sedeno, a Jesuit architect, to construct the fortress," Colonel Oliver informed them, obviously delighting himself in sharing his knowledge of the historic grounds. "It took a hundred and forty-nine years and three governors to complete the job."

They walked through rows of rock columns, up a short flight of stairs, and entered a brick building.

"This is Jose Rizal's prison cell," the colonel said.

Taylor remembered reading of Rizal, the great Filipino patriot executed by the Spanish.

"It was here he wrote Me Ultima Adios, or My Last Farewell," Oliver said.

Morris Day motioned to Taylor and pointed to a bronze plaque on the wall. He read aloud the words, "Nothing then will it matter to place me in oblivion...I go where no slaves are, no butchers, no oppressors, where faith cannot kill, where God is the sovereign Lord."

Oliver said, "The day after he wrote the verse he was shot. His farewell message was hidden in his dishes and later found by his friends. It was printed and distributed to the people and fanned the flames of independence and freedom."

When the young chaplains completed the tour, they were impressed with Manila's grandeur and anxious to see more. Finally they settled in their quarters just outside the walled city.

From his billet, Taylor could see the National Congress Hall and the presidential offices. As he looked out over the beautiful city, it seemed a long way from Henderson, Texas, and the Sabine River where he had fished during the summer as a boy.

His father, William Louis Taylor, ran a nursery, and that meant work. It didn't leave much time for fishing, but Preston had a favorite fishing hole and went there as often as possible. There was also the land to be cultivated, enough for all seven of the Taylor boys, and Preston, being the biggest, had to lead out.

When his family left Henderson and bought a ranch between Kilgore and Gladewater, the chores increased. Each summer after the perennial spells of malaria, he plowed, built fences, hunted rabbits and stole a few minutes for a swim in the creek.

He learned the mules and their insolent ways. They became his friends, teaching him control and patience. Often he thought it would be easier just to flail one right good, but he soon learned that a soft tone brought better results.

"Treat the mules right and they'll give you an honest day's work," Dad Taylor had often instructed, and he was nearly always right.

Taylor saw himself back on the ranch, following Muley and Sol down the long furrows, watching the rain clouds on the horizon, smelling the grass and broken ground."

"Chaplain Lieutenant Robert Preston Taylor," he whispered, "the preacher." The word lingered in his mind. Preachers had been big men in his life. The little Methodist back in Gladewater, he remembered, was a stem-winder. Preston was only fourteen when he attended that preacher's revival meeting. His own folks were all Baptists, but that didn't matter much in East Texas. The Baptists and Methodists, a few Disciples, and even an occasional Catholic, joined in the community meetings in Sabine. Everyone but the Campbellites. They weren't "joiners." And they didn't like piano music, Jew's harp, musical saw – they were against them all.

"That Methodist preacher can't be more than twenty-five," he had heard his mother, Holly Jane, say at breakfast one morning. The perceptive, big-hearted woman sensed that the preacher had almost talked Preston into becoming a believer during that meeting, Preston had really wanted to believe, but he didn't understand his own feelings, so he decided to wait until the next summer, when the revival would shift to the Joy Baptist Church, a few miles west of Sabine.

It was a big day for the Taylor family when the revival started. Preston had been thinking about becoming a Christian for a long time. When the Reverend M. E. Luper finished preaching, he invited the congregation to make any commitment they wanted to make to God. Preston quietly stepped away from his seat and went down the aisle.

It had really been a grand experience, as though a deep sense of personal guilt had been removed from his soul. Mom had joined him at the altar, and was hugging him and crying. V. L. and Daffin and Russell stopped playing tag in the back of the church. When they saw Mom crying at the altar, they were afraid Pres-ton had surrendered to be a foreign missionary or something.

Preston felt clean inside following the experience. But he became a little uneasy when Reverend Luper came by and said, "Boy, someday God may call you to preach, and you'll do it."

The revival ended and many of the people left, not to return until the following summer. But not Pres-ton Taylor. He was in church every Sunday, and everywhere he went he told his friends of his new experience. The preacher asked him to teach a Sunday-school class, and the old ladies in the church prophesied that Preston would someday be a great preacher second only to George W. Truett of Dallas.

One night during prayer meeting, a deacon called on him to pray in public. He froze, unable to think of anything to say. His legs were on the verge of buckling, when he remembered the opening words of the Lord's Prayer. He began, "Our Father, which art in heaven." Then he couldn't think of the second line. He stammered a little, then continued with his own prayer. "We bless our God for church and home, for sun and rain, for work and freedom. We thank our God for our church where we can worship and lean of our Christian heritage. We thank Thee, our God, that we can live as free men, free from the chains of tyranny that would try to enslave man's conscience. But more than anything, else, we thank Thee, our God, for your Son, Jesus Christ, who came to earth to set men free. Thank you for setting us free, in Jesus' name, Amen." It was his first public prayer, and everyone who heard its simplicity and felt its warmth knew he would someday be a preacher. He looked up and saw his mother, sitting three rows in front of him, wipe a tear from her eye.

During the following months he spent hours reading the Bible. Abraham, Moses, Samson, Peter, John, Paul – all heroes of the faith became real characters, and he recognized parallels in his own life. It soon became apparent to everyone, including Preston, that God was calling him into the Gospel ministry.

One day his mother called him into the kitchen and asked him to sit down on the bench by the long wooden table.

"Preston, your father and I have been doing a lot of thinking and praying. If you're really serious about becoming a preacher boy, we think you ought to go to the Baptist Academy in Jacksonville for your last two years of high school."

The wrinkles beside her eyes formed little arcs as she smiled. "We've saved some money for your schooling. If you want to go, you can."

She stood and turned toward the big cook stove, lifted the heavy iron lid from the front and added several sticks of wood to the fire. Then, with her apron she wiped tears from her eyes, turned again and said, "Well, boy, what's it going to be?"

He couldn't talk. His heart began to pound and his throat became dry. Of course, he wanted to become a preacher boy, he told himself, but leaving the farm and V. L. and Daffin and all the people down at the church would be plenty hard.

He bowed his head and prayed silently. He would trust God to help him make the important decision. He waited several minutes, then replied, "Mom, I want to go. It's God's will." His mother put her arms around the tall, red-headed boy and hugged him gently. "Now go tell your father. We've got work to do. School starts next week."

All the family escorted him down the lane to the rural route postbox where the last good-bys were said. Then he stepped into the bus and was on his way to Jacksonville.

During the next two summers he returned home and worked with his brothers on the farm. But when he entered Jacksonville Junior College, he was so busy preaching he seldom got home.

In 1920, at the beginning of the Depression, hundreds of students dropped out of school. But the Taylor farm held out, and Preston made plans to enter Baylor

University to complete his college training. Baylor was the Promised Land to Texas Baptist preacher boys. Not only did it have the best Bible department in the Southwest, it also gave scholarships to young preachers.

His days of preparation passed like a panorama before his eyes. He felt the years had gone too quickly, even seminary and graduate school. And Ione. Dear, beautiful Ione.

He wondered what she was doing at that very moment. Her presence was so real he felt he could almost reach out and touch her long, flowing black hair or place his freckled hands around her thin, girlish waistline. For a fleeting moment, he could see her seated in the third pew on the left – where she always sat to listen to her husband preach. Her sympathetic smile, he thought, had always been so encouraging.

He remembered the day she said she would marry him he felt like the happiest and luckiest guy in the graduate school at the seminary. Tall, slim, beautiful Ione. My dear Ione, oh my Lord how I miss you, he thought.

She had been the only one in his family to bid him bon voyage at the port of San Francisco when the USAT Washington sailed. The days together prior to sailing had been beautiful. Now he found himself wishing his year's tour of duty in the Philippines would pass quickly so he could return to Ione.

Had it been only yesterday – that spring day when his Mom and Dad got off the trolley out near Seminary Hill in Fort Worth to attend his last graduation – it couldn't have been clearer. They had been to Baylor for the ceremonies and to Fort Worth two years earlier, when he had completed his regular minister's course. Now the time had come to receive his doctorate in theology and he soon would be taking Ione to the Hickory Grove Baptist Church near Kilgore, where he would serve as pastor. He was prepared to straddle Rosinante and charge the traditional Baptist windmills.

That day had been memorable. As the faculty from the school of theology marched down the center of the crowded auditorium, he breathed a prayer of thanksgiving for having had the opportunity to study with them.

When the registrar called Robert Preston Taylor, doctor of theology, he stepped proudly to the center of the platform. Dr. L. R. Scarborough, the seminary president, placed the red cape over his head and whispered, "We're very proud of you, boy." And Dr. Conner, who had always told the boys not to be afraid to think because their minds wouldn't shock God, smiled his approval.

The days at Hickory Grove had been exciting, but it wasn't long before the Little Flock Church in the neighboring county called Taylor. Since it was larger and promised a wider ministry, he said farewell to Hickory Grove.

His reputation as an outstanding pulpiteer was spreading throughout Texas, and in 1938 the South Fort Worth Baptist Church asked him to come as pastor. He wasn't sure he was ready for such a large church, but after careful prayer, and with Ione's encouragement, he accepted.

The new pastorate made many demands on the young preacher. Hospital calls, committee meetings, speaking to civic clubs, home-to-home visitation and sermon preparation took most of his time and energy.

One day in the spring of 1938, he received a letter from the Chaplain's Division of the War department, asking him to spend part of his summer ministering to the troops in the camps. He had heard of the troop buildup, but he hadn't realized there was a shortage of army and navy chaplains. He decided to accept a commission in the Army Reserve, and spent several weeks in July and August working with the troops in Fort Hood, near San Antonio.

He saw young boys, many just out of high school, being molded into soldiers and trained to fight, if necessary, for their country, and when he returned to his church he couldn't forget the young troopers who seemed to need so much spiritual help. Later, another call came from the War Department asking him to spend a year as an Army Air Corps chaplain ministering to troops somewhere in the Orient. Again, he prayed. Convinced in his heart he should go, he asked the church to grant him a year's leave of absence. He knew the most difficult part of it would be his separation from Ione, but he couldn't get away from the conviction that he should go.

"We'll miss you, Preacher," Brother Thomas, who was sort of the boss deacon, had said when the final announcement was made to the congregation. "But our men out there need all the help they can get. We'll back you up in prayer as you go."

The excursion into his memory ended abruptly as his roommate, Earl Short, entered the room. Captain short was an artillery officer who had been in the Philippines only a short time, but already knew the ropes and readily offered his assistance in getting the new chaplain settled. His little mustache bobbed up and down as he showed Taylor a map of the area and pointed out the mess hall, parade grounds and chapel. Then, since his unit was scheduled for gunnery practice that

afternoon, he left Taylor to his new and lonely surroundings.

In the days that followed, Taylor approached his
work with vigor, carefully planning each phase of his
ministry. He planned two services each Sunday, sometimes more. A midweek prayer meeting was held each
Wednesday in the old theater inside the Cuartel, just
prior to the movie. Sometimes as many as five hundred
men of the Thirty-First attended. Taylor didn't know
whether it was or the service, or the movie, or both. But
they came, and he made certain they received some
message of hope from the Bible. Chaplain William
Dawson, Taylor's closest friend and classmate at Southwestern Seminary, who had returned to Manila from
field exercises with his unit, assisted with the services
and shared the preaching.

During their seminary days everyone called Dawson
"Mussolini," because his bald head made him look so
much like Il Duce. He was generally soft-spoken, but
when he became too excited the redness in his face
slowly crept down his cheeks until it covered even his
neck.

One evening following the service, Taylor invited
Dawson into his office. "Bill," he said. "I want to begin
a service out on B Range."

Dawson shifted his left forefinger back and forth
across his chin and answered, "Sounds great! When do
we begin?"

"Next week. But tonight I wanted you to pray with
me about B Range and all the young men who come
through there," he replied. "If we can get them before
they get into the bars and cabarets, we may be able to
save them a lot of misery."

Both chaplains had heard about the quarantine

camp on B Range, where all the new troopers were de-
tained to make sure no disease broke out. If it did, it
could be contained in that area.

"Yeah," Dawson replied. "We may be able to hit
some pretty good licks before the city lights get in their
eyes."

"They'll never wash away their loneliness with
booze," Taylor said. Dawson agreed.

The two men dropped to their knees and began
praying silently. They recognized the spiritual odds
they faced, but they also knew the source of their own
power.

Taylor went to B Ranger a few days early to get acquainted with all the new troops. The grounds also
doubled as a training center for recruits learning to
handle infantry weapons. He lay in the dust beside a
young boy, encouraging him when his mark was good
and razzing him when he missed. Finally, the boy
handed the Springfield to Taylor.

"Here, Preach, try it yourself."

Taylor took the rifle and made four bull's-eyes in
five shots. He hadn't lost his touch from jackrabbit
shooting days in East Texas.

B Range was a chaplain's heaven. Not only was
there a great challenge, but it offered an ideal atmosphere for getting acquainted with the men. They began
to look on Taylor as their friend and good-naturedly
razzed him at every chance. But they depended on him
in times of loneliness and sadness.

Taylor pitched a big tent in the middle of the recruit
camp and announced the first Sunday morning service.
The response surprised him, and he later admitted to
Chaplain Dawson that his faith had really been a little
weak. Several who went to that first service were mem-

bers of churches back home. For others, it was the first they had ever attended, but all sang lustily.

A sergeant who had some experience in church music hastily organized twenty-five officers and enlisted men into an impromptu choir. A deep hush settled over the tent as they sang, "What a friend we have in Jesus, all our sins and griefs to bear." Heads were bowed, and more than one recruit lifted a handkerchief to his eyes and wiped tears away.

Taylor announced his subject, "The Tragedy of Sin." Every eye in the tent fixed on the red-haired, tall chaplain. He had marched with them in the field, eaten the same C-rations, and slept with them on the ground. They knew he could be trusted. He was one of them.

"Men, the Bible says sin is the root of all the world's problems. It is the root of your personal problems. Sin can take a man and shake him like a dog shakes a snake, but it never lets him go.

"Under conditions here in the Philippines, there are lots of temptations. Manila is full of nightclubs and bars. You can buy most anything, including a lot of trouble. Any man who doesn't have something better may wind up there." He paused and searched their eyes, trying to find responsive ones, then continued, "But there is something better – it's a person, and that person is Christ. His teachings can deliver you in the hour of temptation and fill your hearts with peace. Then you won't need what they're selling down on Dewey Boulevard. You'll be able to live above that. And remember, you'll always feel better tomorrow if you will live by your convictions today."

Like a surgeon's knife, his words cut at the disease of loneliness that plagued so many of the young boys who were so far away from home, away from the morality their families and friends imposed on them. Now they had to stand alone.

After encouraging the boys to be soldiers for the Lord as well as good soldiers for their country, he called for the choir to sing a final hymn. Soon the strains of "O happy day that fixed my choice, On Thee my Savior and my God," filled the tent.

When the service ended, no one left. They sat quietly meditating on the message, their families, the uncertain future. Then, one by one, they stood and walked slowly out of the tent.

The next day, Taylor learned that one of the drill instructors had a Morse code set and could communicate freely with the States. He asked the operator to let the men send messages back to their families. The sergeant consented but asked that each message be cleared by the chaplain, and from then on, Taylor spent part of every day helping the young boys prepare the messages.

A corporal from Virginia asked his mother not to let his brother enlist "till he's 18, cause it's hot out here and Jerry ain't even shavin' yet." Another, a private from California, wrote, "To Mom and Dad. Just wanted to say thanks for everything you've always done for me. I've never said it before, but recently a new light turned on somewhere in my heart."

Joey, a recruit with big floppy ears, addressed his message to Lulu Mall, his girl friend back in North Carolina. "Stay away from Eli Bender," he wrote. "I'll be home in a year or two, and then you'll forget all about Eli."

Troopers of the Thirty-first spread the word – Taylor was a man's man. They were proud of the "Chappie." He understood their failures and was always there to help them put the pieces back together again. They were glad he was there, and so was he.

2.

War!

On Sunday morning, December 7, 1941, hoof beats of the little ponies pulling the calesa carts down the brick street awakened him. After a quick shower, he roused a sleepy Captain Short, just back from two weeks of field exercises, reminded him it was Sunday, and invited him to the evening chapel service.

The choir from the Union Church of Manila had consented to present a sacred music concert. Taylor had been planning the service for weeks, unaware of what it would prepare him for on that historic day.

After preaching at Fort McKinley in the morning and visiting troops in the field during the afternoon, he returned to his own chapel in the Cuartel de Espana for the evening service.

The choir began the service by singing, almost prophetically, "In Christ There Is No East or West." The audience sat spellbound. The melodious words filled searching hearts with long-sought answers. Others reflected on their own spiritual needs, still other on the future – a future that in a few short hours would sweep them up in its turbulence and terror. All knew they were truly in the house of God when, at the close of the service, Taylor said, "Today your sermon was in song. It was preached through these dedicated voices. Before we go, if you have a commitment, a resolve you wish to make to God this day, stand quietly and come here to the altar for prayer."

A Filipino civilian moved first, then a sergeant from the Thirty-first. Several others followed. After dismissing the congregation, Taylor went to the altar and knelt down beside each inquirer, speaking an encouraging word, quoting Scriptures, answering a question. One by one, they approached the end of their quest and found a strange calm. It would sustain them in the pandemonium to come.

An hour passed. Only one figure remained before the altar, an eighteen-year-old boy Taylor had never seen before.

"Is it settled, son?" he asked, placing his hand on his shoulder.

"Yes, Sir, it's been settled for some time," he answered. "I just don't ever want to let go of today." He rose to his feet and sat down in the front pew. "Chaplain, I got to tell you something." He hesitated, dropping his eyes to the carpeted floor. "Some of us fellows, well, we've done some pretty bad things, I guess."

His words of confession didn't come easy. Contrition marked his youthful face. Taylor sat down beside him, ready to listen, should he choose to unload his burden. The soldier's lips moved, but there were no audible sounds.

"Son, you don't have to tell me, you know. If it's between you and the Lord, you can just tell Him."

The boy's eyes flashed toward the chaplain as the words penetrated his conscience. "Yeah, between me and God, and I've already told Him about it and promised to never do it again." A smile raced across his face.

It was late when Taylor arrived back at his quarters.

At 4:30 the next morning, Captain Short bounded into the room, switched on the light and yelled, "Preston! Preston! Wake up! The Japs have hit Pearl Harbor. The war's started!"

It was damp and chilly when the two men walked through the gate of the Walled City and parted, the captain to join his cannoneers, and Taylor to report to Colonel Doane, commander of the Thirty-first. Several other officers had already assembled for the briefing, their faces tense.

The colonel spoke.

"Men, Jap bombers are heading toward Manila, and a convoy has been spotted off the coast of Indo-china. For the next few days we will bivouac in the valley south of McKinley. Prepare your units. Full field gear. Be ready to move on an instant's notice."

Back in his quarters, Taylor stuffed his field clothes into a duffel bag while he listened to the news report from KMZH:

"At seven fifty-five a.m. Hawaii time, about three hundred and sixty Japanese planes attacked the Pacific fleet units at the naval base, and army and air corps units at Hickam Field and other nearby installations. The fleet lost the battleships Arizona, California, Oklahoma and West Virginia, the mine layer Oglala and the target ship Utah.

"The surprise attack also destroyed one hundred and seventy-four American planes and damaged four battleships, three cruisers and three destroyers.

"The office of Fleet Admiral Husband E. Kimmel reports the Pacific Fleet and Hawaii's air defenses were dealt a crippling blow.

"In Tokyo, the militant Japanese High Command immediately declared war on the United States and Great Britain.

"Informed sources in Washington, D. C. expect President Roosevelt tomorrow to ask Congress for a declaration of war against Japan.

"In other news, General Douglas MacArthur has ordered all Philippine Army units into active duty. In a message to the people, President Manuel Quezon urged all Filipinos to be calm and have faith."

Taylor turned off the radio, took a last nostalgic look at the picture of Ione on the dresser, placed it in his army bag, and briskly departed.

As he walked down Isaac Peral Street he saw no signs of pandemonium. Civilians queued up to carretela buses. Blue-uniformed, giggling children skipped and danced past him on their way to school.

The threat of war apparently had not fully dawned on the people in the streets. Many were making final preparations to visit the barrios in the province to celebrate the Feast of the Immaculate Conception.

Suddenly newsboys began to hawk their papers, shrilly screaming, "Binomba ang Pearl Harbor, Binomba ang Pearl Harbor" in their native Tagalog. Then, without warning, the shrill scream of air-raid sirens pierced the streets. Almost automatically, Taylor glanced at his watch. It was 11:27 a.m.

Traffic came to a snarling halt; drivers cursed and pounded their horns. Women with infants strapped to their backs ran helter-skelter, frantically searching for places to hide.

Taylor could see the big red rising sun painted on the wings of the medium-range bombers heading toward the Cavite Naval Base across the bay. Twice they circled the base, then, leveling off, dumped their fiery destruction. An elderly lady crossed herself as flames shot into the sky. A little girl clutched her mother's leg.

Meanwhile, another formation passed over the city

and hit Nichols Field with demolition and incendiary bombs. A thunderous explosion, rocking the area like a gigantic quake, was followed by a thick bank of smoke. Taylor guessed the fuel dump had taken a direct hit.

His hope that the city, with its rich religious and cultural heritage, would be spared soon crumbled, as he saw twenty-seven bombers from another squadron begin bombing army barracks, office buildings and warehouses near the bay. Fire broke out in a hundred places. Sirens and horns were deafening. Teams of firemen, with their antiquated equipment, bravely rushed out to combat the flames, only to find their hoses had been cut by Japanese sympathizers. The tense and fearful crowd viewing the holocaust cheered wildly when an antiaircraft battery scored a hit, and smoke burst from the engine of one of the marauding bombers.

From his position on Isaac Peral Street, Taylor commanded a near-perfect view of the zigzagging merchant ships in the bay, running for their lives. Without air protection, the bay became a death trap as all the ships were destroyed or damaged.

Following each attack, he rushed into the city to help rescue the wounded, using his own jeep and commandeering several others to take the injured to the hospitals. His heart winced when he saw how the Pearl of the Orient had become a heap of rubble. Most of the streets were quiet and deserted. The Luneta, the once beautiful park located adjacent to the Intramuros, was pitted with large craters. The Pasig River, flowing down from the crescent of mountains that surrounded the city, was filled with smoldering debris. Little children, separated from their parents during the height of the melee, cried hysterically.

Mountains of cargo – from undelivered Christmas

packages to grand pianos – were piled on the wharves, as the ships were hastily unloaded. Looters – children, beggars, priests and crippled old men – ransacked the displaced cargo, piling it into carts and hauling it away.

The smell of death, in its various ugly forms, enveloped the streets. Taylor sat down beside the body of a little Filipino boy, gazed through the smoke at the Santo Domingo Cathedral, now only a skeleton of its past splendor, and wept. He had learned his first lesson – war spares neither sacred shrine nor helpless civilians.

Just at the height of the destruction, Taylor suddenly heard the bells from Santo Domingo Cathedral and other churches in the city mournfully tolling against the horrifying sounds of destruction, their foreboding tones passing judgment on the attackers but filling the hearts of the panicky people with peace and calm. For a moment the whole world came to an abrupt halt, as the people strained their eyes to get a glimpse of the spires of their beloved church, half-hidden by smoke and flames.

As he listened to the bells, Taylor realized that, militarily, he was helpless. His ministry must be to the spirit, the morale of the men, and in silent prayer he committed himself to that duty.

Rays from the setting sun were darkened by clouds of smoke still soaring into the sky when Taylor reached his regiment, camped in the small valley just south of Fort William McKinley. The guard on the perimeter was edgy. Troopers of the Thirty-first huddled together and spoke in hushed tones.

After placing his gear in the regimental chaplain's tent, Taylor sent a message to all the company commanders announcing a worship service at 1900 hours. The next few minutes he spent rummaging through the discarded boxes near the mess tent. Finally, he found three orange crates. They would serve as his pulpit.

Dozens of men grouped themselves around the tent entrance, helmets in hand, as the time for the service approached. Taylor could see only profiles silhouetted against the dim glow of coal-oil lanterns placed all around the camp. The troops crowded close together, fearful lest they miss an encouraging word.

The chaplain stood on the crates and read from the Bible, "Let not your heart be troubled: ye believe in God, believe also in me. In my Father's house are many mansions: if it were not so, I would have told you. I go to prepare a place for you." Then he spoke for a few minutes on "Christ in the Hour of Battle," assuring the men they would not face the enemy alone. His optimistic words met anxious hearts and filled them with hope.

At the close of the service, Colonel Doane announced officers' call. Succinctly, he briefed them on the critical situation. Then, tacking a map to a piece of cardboard hanging in the tent, he told them that Mindanao had been bombed that morning, that Aparri had been strafed by Zeroes from Formosa, that his information was that northern Luzon would be next. It was there that the Thirty-first was to be sent. Assignment: the defense of Bataan.

Grim faces greeted the news. Bataan, with its 517 statute miles, had its own reputation. It was what the career men called a "hardship post." Although beautiful beaches with giant coconut palms jutted into Manila Bay from the southwest corner of Luzon, the inland jungle was known as a death hole, filled with every tropical disease known to man.

"You're going to meet a savage enemy," the colonel said. "Meet them like Americans. Dismissed."

Taylor sensed weariness and sadness bordering on pathos in the colonel's tired eyes. A directive committing men to battle is the ultimate decision facing any field commander. His solders are the professional arbiters of fate. His decisions run the spectrum of life and death. His judgment is the final authority, his mistakes are his own. Carrying such a burden was too much for any mortal. It required a touch of the supernatural.

As Taylor reached the door of the tent, he hesitated, certain the commander wanted to talk. His intuition was right.

"Chaplain Taylor, got a minute?" He turned abruptly and went to the desk where the colonel was seated, thumbing through a stack of papers.

"Your first battle, isn't it?" the colonel asked, looking up from his paperwork. "In the last war there was a young chaplain."

"What was his name, sir?"

"Don't remember his name, just remember him." For several minutes neither spoke. The colonel appeared to be in deep thought, as though recalling the lost lives entangled in the heroics and tragedies of the war supposedly fought to end all wars. "It was cold in the trenches, no heat, the blankets were wet. Our morale hit rock bottom. I was just a raw lieutenant and wanted to give up. Then one day I saw that chaplain, down on his knees in the mud. It did something to me – and it pulled me through."

Taylor could think of nothing to say. He felt that any attempt to reduce his feelings to words would destroy both. Yet he yearned to express the deep respect he felt for the aged commander.

"That's all, Lieutenant. You'll be all right. When the going gets rough, remember to pray. And read your

Bible to the troops. We'll not survive unless you do.

"Thank you, Colonel. I'll remember that." Taylor stood to leave.

"By the way, you'll need a jeep and a driver. I'm assigning Corporal Denny. He can also serve as your assistant.

"But, Colonel, the vehicles …" He knew of the shortage of personnel carriers.

"It's yours, Lieutenant. As long as we have one jeep, it will be available for you to visit and pray with the troops."

3.

BATAAN

Three days later, troops of the Thirty-first broke camp, joined a ragged convoy of army trucks and headed for Bataan. Taylor and his driver, Marvin Denny, were among the first to join the line, leaving the security of old Fort McKinley to begin their odyssey into all the uncertainties of Bataan.

By midday the vanguard reached a point on the Pelar-Bagac Trail running from Manila Bay west to the South China Sea. The enchantment of the lush tropical growth, the stately coconut trees and the wide-fronded banana-tree branches, enraptured the troops, temporarily taking their minds off the humid, stifling heat.

Their orders said they were to set up roadblocks and maintain the security of the two main coastal roads, known simple as the East and West. Running south down both sides of the hostile peninsula, they converged at Mariveles, the center of the Service Command Area in the south. Company commanders assembled their platoon leaders, ordering them to begin the defense preparations. Taylor grabbed a shovel and joined a squad digging foxholes, then helped another stretch barbed wire in front of the newly dug foxholes. Trenches and gun emplacements were also being prepared. Soon the hillside was honeycombed with revetments. The strategists of what was now known as Operation Orange 3 vowed that the Pelar-Bagac Line would hold indefinitely, if the troops could receive adequate logistical support. The tropical jungle, with its varied shades of dark green and brown, offered a natural camouflage to provide protection for the troops from Japanese planes. The forest and the rugged terrain also would slow down all the enemy's mechanized columns, forcing him to rely on horses and foot soldiers. The road across the interior could be used for supply lines and troops maneuvering from one front to the other.

The Japanese began their ground attack on Luzon on December 10, with amphibious landings at Appari in the south and Vigan in the north. However, they held back any major offensive. There were reports of widely scattered "brush fires," but no major battles had developed during the first week of the war. Taylor sensed a growing restlessness among the troops in his regiment.

Knowing that the men needed to think less, talk more, he decided to visit each foxhole up and down the line. He called Corporal Denny, instructed him to bring the jeep around, and headed down the line. As he approached each unit, he was greeted by the usual, "Hi Preach! What you doin' out of church?" After visiting briefly with each squad, he opened his New Testament, and in the midst of the hush that transformed the moss-carpeted jungle into a great outdoor cathedral, he read what experience had taught him were their favorite passages. Then, after prayer and another brief chat, he and Denny moved to the next unit.

Since the troopers of the Thirty-first were already fortified and waiting for the assault, they had time on their hands. Ingeniously, they constructed their fox-holes for maximum luxury. Coley, a crusty old beer-bellied sergeant from Missouri, carefully built a little roof over his foxhole, bracing it with bamboo poles and covering it with leaves from the spreading mango trees. Big John, a corporal from Alabama, had been a weight lifter who had joined the army to see the world. He had scrounged a piece of sheet metal from a passing convoy, shaped it with his bare hands and made an A-frame cover for his foxhole. His friends called it "The Chalet."

As the jeep chugged back into the base camp, Corporal Denny was so tired he could barely stand. He pulled up beside a straw-colored giant malaikmo tree with its pinkish-buff trunk. Taylor spread his blanket on the ground and lay down to review the events of the past few hours.

Still no attack came. The Thirty-first, attached to General Wainwright's I Corps, waited in readiness as the Japanese High Command coolly calculated the final attack that would seal the doom of the defenders of Bataan.

Then without warning and under the deceptive cover of a gray dawn, it began. A huge invasion force landed at Lingayen Gulf in three transport echelons – six divisions, eighty thousand men. Colonel Doane was alerted and ordered to move his men from the Pelar-Bagac Trail to Mabutang area. There his troops would cover the retreat of II Corps from Manila and the central plains, while elements of the North Luzon force would seek to parry the frontal assault. Taylor joined the forced march.

It was getting dark when the regiment's vanguard reached their new positions, two miles north of Abucay. Again they began digging in. Taylor was swinging a pickax when he heard footsteps from behind. Turning, he saw Corporal Denny. "Marvin, need something?"

"Chaplain, this just ain't right."

"Oh, like what?"

"You know…this is Christmas Eve."

The words hit Taylor like a bolt of lightning. Ten thousand miles from home, he had been so totally involved in ministering to the army and in the rudiments of struggle and survival, he had forgotten the day. His guilt temporarily troubled him, then passed, as he realized that the true meaning of Christmas was serving others.

"Yeah, Marvin, it's Christmas Eve and something ain't right," he replied, emphasizing the "ain't."

Then he began to sing: "Silent Night, Holy Night. All is calm, all is bright." A squad close by heard the soft words. They, too remembered the day and joined in, and soon the entire front line at Abucay echoed the carol they had known from childhood.

At 9 a.m. the following morning, Colonel Doane scheduled a briefing for officers and non-coms. Morris Day had just arrived from Mabutang and walked with Taylor to the briefing. They assembled in the old church in the nearby barrio. The once stately roof had been destroyed in the bombings and its wooden rafters were charred. Colonel Doane entered, accompanied by another tall, erect colonel. The men stood and saluted.

"Men, this is Colonel Steele, ranking officer in the Thirty-first. Today he is assuming command. I will be his adjutant."

"At ease men. Today we plan the defense of Abucay. But first, there is something else. Today is Christmas. Our loved ones in the States are already celebrating. Although we're engaged in hostilities with the enemy and digging positions of defense, we'll pause for a Christmas religious service. The chaplains will now conduct the service." At his command, the men removed their steel helmets and sat down on the dirt floor of the church.

Chaplain Day, standing erect, a slight smile on his bony face, stepped forward and read the record of Christ's birth from the New Testament. Then he prayed, "Lord, that simple birth tells us so much about God – your love, your concern, your help. Today we rely on you as we defend our country, to live lives of victory, to face all our tomorrows like Americans, like Christians. Today we give ourselves to Thee. Amen." Eloquently spoken, Taylor thought. But Morris Day had always been eloquent – as a college debate star and as an outstanding young preaching student at Southwestern Seminary.

A squadron of Japanese bombers roared across the peninsula and bombed some distant target as Taylor stood and walked to the center of the group of officers and men. Their attention had remained steadfast. "Christ was born to inaugurate an era of peace. But many nations do not know peace, because they, as yet, do not know the Christ of peace. Christ came to change man's heart. Then his actions will find their proper pursuit. Then war will cease. Then, only then, will peace reign." As his eyes searched the men's faces, there was so much he wanted to say – how they could know peace in time of conflict, hope in time of despair, comfort in time of fear. But he sensed they knew it, too.

Their faces told him they did. "This was all made possible by one who died on a Roman cross, but who also walks with us today at Abucay as our Savior." He sat down.

Colonel Steele added, "Around the person of Christ revolves the principles on which our nation was built. May the day never come when our families and loved ones will not be able to worship and celebrate this day in freedom."

As the officers began their briefing, Day and Taylor left the church for a tour of the regiment. Corporal Denny, a broad smile across his face, carried a satchel full of New Testaments for all the men who wanted one.

The younger men good-naturedly greeted the chaplains with, "Oh, oh, here comes the angel patrol," or "Put away the girlie books, the saints are marching in." Another yelled, "Pass the turkey, Preach! And some cranberry sauce and dressing!" The chaplains joined in the laughter, happy the boys could still laugh, but then the joking ceased and the men listened as the two chaplains, alternating with each detachment, read the Christmas story, prayed, and moved on down the line. Corporal Denny followed, distributing New Testaments. By nightfall, they had visited the entire unit.

The East highway leading past Abucay was bumper to bumper with various military vehicles and carreletas and calesas carrying frightened Filipinos south. Colonel Steele deployed a battalion around the Calumpit Bridge near Layac Junction at the neck of the peninsula to cover the retreating armies. Taylor also accompanied the detachment. Colonel Steele's intelligence reports showed two invading armies – one from San Fernando Pampanga in the east, the second from Clark Field in the north.

Taylor watched the tanks, guns, trucks and masses of men as they crossed the bridge. They carried their field packs, bandoleers of ammunition, and an occasional chicken or goose. When all the American and Filipino units were safely on Bataan, U. S. Army engineers blew the bridge. The North Luzon force, bruised and battered, had fought parrying actions, holding until the enemy deployed a sizable force, then retreating, dynamiting bridges behind them. This battle pattern – stand and fight, retreat and dynamite – was repeated over and over.

One of the last vehicles to cross the bridge was an army ambulance with a large red cross painted on the side. Taylor flagged it down, opened the rear door and climbed in as the ambulance continued down the curving road toward Abucay. Inside, Taylor found four patients on canvas litters, two deep on either side, and a medic who was steadying a bottle of plasma held loosely in a crude stand. His fatigues were covered with dried, caked blood.

"What's your name, soldier?" Taylor asked one of the wounded, a boy whose face was pale and gaunt.

"Tommy, sir. Call me Tommy."

Taylor pulled a handkerchief from his pocket, dampened it with water from his canteen, and gently wiped the boy's forehead.

"How old are you, Tommy?" he asked, trying to detract the boy's attention from his pain.

"Nineteen – well, nearly."

The medic handed the bottle of plasma to Taylor and began examining the other patients.

"This one's dead," he whispered, pulling a blanket over another man's face. "If we don't get off this damn road, we'll lose them all."

With his free hand, Taylor opened his New Testament and slowly began reading:

"For God so loved the world
That he gave His only begotten Son,

That whosoever believeth in Him
Should not perish,
But have everlasting life."

When the ambulance reached Abucay, Taylor began making preparations for the first funeral service to be conducted on Bataan.

He called Chaplain Day, who had been working in the crudely erected hospital near the colonel's tent, and together they fashioned a cross from two pieces of board taken from a rations box. Carefully they wrapped the dead soldier in Taylor's blanket, tied it with hemp, and carried it to a little slope near the edge of the bivouac area.

Taylor removed his shirt and began digging the grave while Day went in search of Ernest Norquest, the regimental bugler.

Ten minutes later, Day returned with the bugler. Taylor put his shirt back on and gently lowered the body into the grave. Then after taps had been sounded, Taylor opened his Bible and read,

"Behold I show you a mystery,
We shall not all sleep, but we shall
All be changed.
O death, where is thy sting?
O grave, where is thy victory?
But thanks be to god, which giveth
the victory
Through our Lord Jesus Christ."

Officers and men of the regiment assembled for an early breakfast on the first Sunday of the battle for Bataan. The sun had not yet risen, but birds chirped in the moss-bearded trees that towered over the dense terrain. Colonel Steele stepped out of his tent.

"Men, today is Sunday. The mess is ready, but before we eat, Chaplain Taylor will lead us in prayer and conduct a brief service."

Taylor stood beside Colonel Steel and began to pray as the men removed their helmets.

"Our Father which art in heaven,
Hallowed be thy name."

Still smarting from their retreat, the men leaned on their rifles as he continued:

"Thy kingdom come,
Thy will be done.
On earth, as it is in heaven."

Spontaneously, the colonel joined him, and soon the surrounding jungle vibrated with the Lord's Prayer carried by a chorus of deep male voices. There were no comfortable pews for these men, no beautiful altar before which they could bow in prayer, but in all his life, Taylor had never witnessed a greater feeling of the presence of the Master. He knew the message of hope had taken hold.

The jaws of the Japanese military pincer began to close as their armies staged a massive frontal assault against the Thirty-first on the battle line near the Abucay Hacienda, an old Spanish estate. Nearby, a cluster of nipa huts housed a small community of Filipino sugar cane workers.

Taylor's jeep pulled up in front of the first-aid station near the main road. Lines of civilians, as far as his eye could see, sought the protection of the American army. They carried pigs, chickens, and little bundles of personal belongings swinging on poles. A small barefoot girl, clutching a rag doll, looked at Taylor and called, "Hi, Joe," probably the only English words she knew. His eyes followed her until she disappeared up the winding road into the mountains. Then he entered the aid station and assisted Lieutenant Donald Reider, one of the regimental surgeons, bandage wounds, treat burns, and load the litter and shock patients into old buses commandeered to move them to the field hospitals in the south.

Taylor discovered the slender, articulate doctor had boundless energy. Together they worked in and out of the trenches.

Under cover of withering artillery fire and dive-bombers, raining destruction from the air, the Japanese infantry moved into position and readied their at-tack on Abucay. The artillery ceased, and for a few minutes a deathly quiet prevailed all along the front. Then with shouts of "Banzai! Banzai!" wave after wave of infantry brigades began the frontal attacks. The defenders, well entrenched in bunkers protected by barbed wire, sprayed the attackers with machine-gun fire and sent them reeling back.

The day was temporarily saved, but soon the Japanese officers, waving samurai swords and screaming at their men, ordered them back into the lines.

Taylor and Reider continued to help the wounded in the bunkers, evacuating the worst cases, collecting dog tags of the dead. Thirty yards away they could see writhing bodies of the Japanese entangled in the barbed-wire defenses. Other troops used these bodies to catapult over the defense structure, only to be caught in a deadly crossfire of American 50-caliber machine guns and rifles.

When it looked as though the defenses would crack, Taylor picked up a wounded man, threw him over his shoulder and headed for the aid station in the rear. Looking back, he could see the positions being overrun, and for a moment he watched as a platoon from the Thirty-first, their ammunition gone, waged hand-to-hand combat with the screaming Japanese infantrymen. Then the assault stopped.

Taylor joined a corpsman going back into no man's land to evacuate the wounded. The sight of the injured men sickened him and he retched. Some wore the ghostly, skeleton like mask of death, their eyes staring blankly at the ground as they staggered. Others crawled or hobbled along, using rifles or bamboo poles as crutches.

Taylor found a lieutenant lying with a broken leg. The man had crawled as far as he could before he had fainted. Taylor improvised a crude splint, placed it on the crushed leg, and carried the injured solder back to friendly lines.

It was difficult to distinguish the living from the dead, but across no man's land he saw a bizarre scene – five unmistakably dead men whose machine-gun nest had taken a direct mortar hit.

Taylor headed toward them only to be stopped by Lieutenant John Prey. Commander of the evacuation detail, Pray pointed out that to go to the nest was sure death, but Taylor would not give up. With two volunteers, he moved toward the lifeless forms fifty yards away. Troops all along the new defense line watched them as they ran, certain their doom was sealed. Taylor himself expected to hear a machine-gun burst any minute, but none came. As the detail approached the dead men, the smell of burnt flesh nauseated the two younger boys. One vomited.

The head had been blown off one of the dead men, and blood trickled from the neck. A piece of flesh dangled limply from a cluster of tangled vines. Clothes were charred, faces badly disfigured. The chaplain fashioned a litter from parts of two shirts, and while one of the volunteers covered their withdrawal, Taylor and the third man carried the corpse back to their own lines, and then returned to retrieve the second and third man. But just as they prepared to lift the last body onto the litter, they spotted a Japanese patrol approaching from a jungle trail. Lieutenant Prey ordered his men to fire on the patrol, and the troops cheered as the detail safely brought in the last body.

"You really caused me some uneasy moments, Chaplain." It was Colonel Steele, a broad grin breaking through the surface of his grimy face. "I'm recommending you for the Silver Star."

Taylor looked around for the two boys who had helped him, hoping the colonel would commend them as well, but they were gone. There were other battles to be fought, men to evacuate, deaths to die.

Taylor instructed Corporal Denny to dig only one grave. The five men had lived together, died as one. Now they would be buried in a common grave.

No one back home would ever know how they died. There would be visions of heroic deaths, and some would probably speculate on how the men died in the arms of their friends, with fulfillment and even peace written on their faces. But Taylor knew differently. Often, when hit, they would scream and claw the ground with their fingers. Some prayed for death that might still be hours away.

Under the cover of heavy darkness, the Thirty-first withdrew to their former positions along the Pelar-Bagac line. From well-fortified entrenchments, patrols surprised and harassed the enemy, then withdrew to the safety of their own lines.

Spearhead elements of the Japanese forces once again prepared for a massive frontal assault against the American lines, and their planes dropped leaflets urging the Americans to surrender. The soldiers used the leaflets to light cigarettes, scribble notes to their wives and sweethearts, and even for toilet paper, a scarce commodity on Bataan.

Colonel Steele was ordered to the south to lead a regiment of air-force ground personnel and was replaced by Colonel Brady.

The next day, waves of shock troops again hurled themselves at the American lines along the West Road. Another combat team swung to the east, cutting off most of the Pelar-Bagac road dividing the peninsula.

Colonel Brady quickly ordered a counterattack, temporarily throwing them back, but he knew the situation was slowly deteriorating. Casualties were high for both sides. The stench of the decaying bodies, exposed to the tropical sun, was so strong no one could eat.

Colonel Brady gave Taylor an army truck and assigned him to Graves Registration's burial detail. As energetically as he had worked with the living, he now worked with the dead. The first day, he and Corporal Denny wore handkerchiefs over their faces to relieve the smell of the dead, but it helped very little. Then they tried gas masks, but the stench still remained in their nostrils.

Japanese bombers continued pounding the American positions. Mortars and howitzers also hit the lines. The once beautiful trees and vegetation around the battle area turned to cinders.

As Taylor and Denny drove down the line, picking up the dead, they spoke words of encouragement to groups of men huddled in their defense positions. Some cowered, others wept.

They reminded Taylor of frightened sheep without a shepherd. But he knew their heroic efforts must be ranked high on the scale of human endurance, although it was becoming quite evident there was a limit to how much a man, any man, could take. Courage, they soon discovered, was not enough to stop a battery of Japanese 105s.

During lulls in the fighting, Taylor conducted brief religious services. He wrote words of favorite hymns on scraps of paper and passed them out to the men. After singing one or two verses with the men, he read a passage of scripture, prayed, and then moved on.

Everywhere he went -- all up and down the line -- he urged the men to surrender their hearts to God, and dozens responded. The following Sunday he baptized fifteen converts in the Alagan River while guards stood by protecting them from Japanese patrols.

With the passing of each day the situation became more critical. Taylor knew the hungry, sick, emaciated troops couldn't continue much longer. Malaria had spread like wildfire. Both hospitals between Mariveles and Cabcaben overflowed. The soldiers were so tired they had to stand to stay awake. Food, already rationed, had been cut by fifty percent, forcing them to eat mangoes and raw bamboo shoots. When the remaining twenty-six cavalry horses and pack mules had been eaten, they hunted monkeys and cobras.

Traveling on the back roads, playing hide-and-seek with Japanese Zeroes, Taylor forced his truck up and down the jagged mountains, through the mosquito-infested jungles, and across rivers in order to be with his men. He often wondered why the Japanese wanted Bataan – so poor, infertile and inhospitable.

Each time he crossed the peninsula he noticed more and more troop movements south toward the hospitals. In a few more days, he figured, their ammunition would be exhausted and rations gone. He also learned that Dr. Reider had used his last quinine. Hundreds of troops, in the first stages of malaria, begged for medicine, but the doctor was helpless.

Early one morning while en route to visit the battalion defending the left flank, a Zero, skimming the trees, spotted Taylor's truck. The pilot climbed, circled the vehicle and swooped down, spraying machine-gun fire. Taylor and Denny jumped into the underbrush. The Zero's flaming guns barked again. Dust jumped up around the truck. Then a bullet hit the gas tank and it exploded. During the long walk back to the command post, Corporal Denny kept wondering about the chaplain – wondering if maybe he led a charmed life.

Just before daylight they arrived back at the command post, exhausted. Minutes later a courier approached Taylor with the message that the colonel wanted to see him.

The colonel's headquarters buzzed with radio reports from the various units. Maps and papers hung on the crude bulletin board made from torn cardboard boxes. The colonel's bunk – in the corner of the tent – hadn't been slept in for three day.

As Taylor entered the tent the colonel, talking to two

of his staff, broke the conversation and turned to the chaplain.

"I heard about your truck. Close call."

"We're still fighting, Colonel. That counts for something," Taylor replied, trying to cover his own fears. He was not ashamed of fear, for he was neither coward nor hero but a mortal, subject to all the uncertainties of life. Yet he knew the morale in the command was fading rapidly. Someone had to hold on as long as possible.

"Chaplain, the gas ration is getting smaller and smaller, but as long as it lasts, use my jeep," Colonel Brady said. "Continue in your work, son. This is our most critical hour."

He paused. "By the way, Lieutenant, you're now promoted to captain."

As Taylor shook hands with the others officers in the command post, a report came over the radio that the enemy had overrun the left flank and was heading directly toward their position.

The battle grew worse day by day. A full retreat was ordered. Colonel Brady knew that two thirds of his forces were sick, and intelligence reported that five thousand fresh Japanese troops were being committed to the battle.

All across the island the Americans fell back. Field commanders were ordered to destroy all weapons that could not be withdrawn, and men, reluctantly obeying, threw firing pins into the dense jungle, bent gun barrels around tree trunks, and destroyed truck engines with armor-piercing shells fired at point-blank range.

As Taylor and Denny rode in the rear of Colonel Brady's jeep, he told them General MacArthur had been ordered to Australia and General Wainwright given the

Philippine command.

The narrow road that led from Cabcaben toward Mariveles was jammed with men struggling to carry their wounded buddies on litters, and stragglers wandered aimlessly, slowly down the jungle paths, some wearing nothing but underwear.

But Colonel Brady was proud of the tiny skeletal force that remained. The few replacements he had received were from all branches of the service, and many had had no infantry training. But they were prepared to die in their foxholes, and by some miracle they still held out although on every other front the Japanese had captured all the strategic points.

Taylor joined the regiment's counterattack. He watched the men move out of their positions, then, one after another, drop from exhaustion a few feet away. The counterattack failed.

That night the Philippine sky turned to a three-dimensional hell in Technicolor as the munitions dumps, about to fall into enemy hands, were destroyed. The Thirty-first received the full brunt of a Japanese aerial bombardment and pounding from the field artillery. Taylor wondered how they could continue to hold out. He knew that unless they surrendered it would be mass murder – but the American flag still flew over the beleaguered peninsula.

One day, Captain Willie Farrell led his company, greatly decimated, past the battalion headquarters. His ammunition almost gone and with no food, he returned to the command post for orders. Tall and erect, his once muscular body showed signs of malnutrition. But like his father, he was a West Pointer and still the picture of a tough fighting man.

Taylor walked over to where he sat and handed him

a small tin of fish, one of his last, and then sat down beside him on the moss at the base of a malabunga tree. From where they sat they could see the waves of Manila Bay.

Willie spoke first: "Chaplain, only recently some of us have learned to live our religion." He paused for a moment, gazed at the bay and continued: "Everything is vanished, gone. But some things are eternal – love, hope faith. When everything else is gone, there's God. You taught us that, Chaplain, and proved it with your life."

The leathery-faced captain placed his arm over his eyes, concealing tears. After the war his diary would be delivered by a friend to Colonel Lewis Farrel, his father. In it Willie had written: "I have just finished reading the Twenty-third Psalm Christ has not promised that we will not meet death, but he has promised to be with us when it comes." Later, on a prison ship en route to Japan, he starved to death.

Easter Sunday, the Thirty-first moved into a reserve position just east of Mount Sumat. During the day, Taylor visited various battalions, speaking individually and to small groups of men. As they waited for orders to move back into the battle zone, he saw several of them reading their pocket New Testaments.

All day the Japanese forward elements continued their heavy push. Their commanders even sent additional aircraft to join the bomber squadrons that already darkened the sky over Mount Sumat, but late in the afternoon the fighting ceased temporarily. The jungle, though covered with dust, smoke and floating particles from the battlefield, suddenly became deathly quiet, and just after sunset Colonel Brady assembled his officers for a final briefing. He asked Taylor to pray, and standing in a circle under the bright moonlight, the officers bowed their heads.

As Taylor left, he prayed again and thanked God for a Christian commander like Colonel Brady who had taken time – even in the hour of battle – to pray for his men.

That night as they drove across the mountains looking for the wounded, Corporal Denny grabbed Taylor's arm. "Chaplain, up there in the sky! It's the Southern Cross!"

Taylor looked and saw the beautiful cross hovering over Bataan.

"Yeah, Marvin. It's a reminder in the north and the south of Christ, the only one who will ever bring our convulsing world to its knees."

He believed what he said, yet the contrast with the fighting and killing on Bataan frightened him. He knew the message of truth had not yet covered the earth.

Committed to battle, the regiment could only give token resistance. Trees, roads, fences and the military defenses were blown to bits. Colonel Brady ordered the final retreat, and the regiment pulled away from the front lines.

That evening Taylor stood on the banks of the San Jacinto River and watched a company of men cross the shallow stream. Although they tried to use a row of rocks in the river as a bridge, many were so weak they slipped and fell into the water. Taylor himself felt a little weak and dizzy, but he was able to muster his strength enough to carry a wounded soldier across the stream.

The battle for Bataan came rapidly to an end, and on March 7 the Thirty-first crumbled and began their retreat through the dense jungles toward Mariveles. From daylight until late into the night the defeated army struggled through the tangled vines. Snakes slithered under their feet, but the air, fragrant with perfumed sweetness from the tropical flowers, was a welcome reprieve from the smell of death. Exotic bushes, growing in multi-colored splendor on the moss-carpeted jungle floor, were filled with fireflies, and blackplumaged birds, frightened at the sound of the strange band of human intruders, flew from tree to tree.

When the stragglers reached Limay Valley, Tay-lor joined the crew working in the first-aid station. A mess truck was set up nearby and as the men arrived, tired, hungry, discouraged, and many of them sick, he hurried to them with hot coffee, soup and a little rice. Some were too weary to eat.

Morale hit rock bottom. The darkest hour ever faced by American soldiers had cast its shadow across their pathway. Taylor knew they soon would face the final mortification – surrender.

Groups of men – restless and nervous – camped around the aid station. Some smoked, others talked of the impending capitulation.

Taylor could not sleep. He went from group to group, serving coffee, giving aid, and calling the men to quietness by leading them in devotion and prayer.

The night was hectic – all troops were moving to the rear. Roads were jammed with vehicles, and the demolition of munitions being destroyed under the shadows of darkness shook the earth.

Captain Reider and Taylor worked feverishly caring for the wounded. Finally, the doctor told Taylor that if the most serious cases were not taken to Baguio, they would die. Sixty-five men to be moved – but how?

The chaplain left the aid tent and called Denny. Just outside of Limay he had seen a deserted bus, apparently out of gas. Carrying two five-gallon auxiliary cans of gas, they hiked down the road to the bus. After emptying the contents into the tank, Denny, choking it like thunder, prepared to crank the engine. "Speak to me, baby. Don't disappoint me now."

He tried the ignition. Nothing.

"This time, baby, this time!"

It cranked, and ten minutes later, the bus was idling in front of the aid station.

They placed the stretcher cases inside, and the ambulatory patients climbed inside.

Field Hospital Number One at Little Baguio was already overflowing, but when the bus arrived, the doctors ingeniously found places for all of the patients and immediately began ministering to them. The doctors directed the second busload to Hospital Number Two, a few miles up the road toward Cabcaben.

With their job completed, the two men returned to the aid station. The bus had to be destroyed, and Taylor told Denny to cut the gas line, fill a bucket and set the fire. But just as the young man returned with a bucket to start the job, Colonel Jack Schwartz, the hospital surgeon, stepped out of the huge tent to ask if the bus would still run. There were about twenty nurses still on Bataan. A boat waited at Mariveles to take them to Corregidor. Would the chaplain get them?

The steep and winding road down to Mariveles was hazardous. Craters, the unmistakable signature of Japanese bombs, often forced the bus to detour from the main road. The nurses, clad in brown khaki uniforms tried to laugh as they spoke of happier times, but underneath they feared the Japanese and what would happen to them if they should fall into enemy hands.

Taylor sat down beside a petite, blond lieutenant with a somber look on her girlish face.

"Well, Lieutenant, leaving Bataan?"

"Yeah, Chaplain. Next stop Corregidor.

"Then what?"

"Who knows? They say there's a big thousand-bed hospital inside Malinta Tunnel."

"By the way, I'm Preston Taylor from Fort Worth, Texas."

"Smiling, she replied, "And I'm Hattie Brantley from Jefferson, Texas. How about that?"

"Jefferson, Texas. I wouldn't have thought of Jefferson, Texas, for the duration."

"Blink your eyes and you miss it when you drive through."

Hattie Brantley watched Taylor as he glanced over his shoulder at the dozen or so other girls scattered through the bus.

"Looking for someone, Chaplain?"

"Well, yes, I am. Is there a Helen Summers in your group?"

"Well, this is your lucky day, Chaplain." Hattie Brantley turned toward the back of the bus. "Helen, hey, Helen, the Chaplain wants to see you."

A short, dark-eyed, beautiful girl, about twenty and dressed in Army fatigues, stood, tried to hold her balance on the careening old bus, then walked toward the front.

"I'm Helen Summers."

"I'll let you two talk," Hattie Brantley said.

"Helen, I'm Chaplain Preston Taylor and I've just come from the battle of Mount Sumat, and . . ." His brief pause quickened her attention.

"Yes, Chaplain?"

"And I met up with this young lieutenant named Benjamin."

"Yes, Arnold Benjamin. We're going to be married when this is all over."

"He's dead, Helen."

"Oh, God, no."

"Yesterday, during the battle for Mount Sumat."

Helen began weeping and coughing. Taylor placed his arm around her and drew her close to him.

"He was a real hero and led his men faithfully throughout the Bataan campaign. And he wanted you to have these."

Reaching into his pocket, he pulled out a gold watch, a key chain and a college ring.

Two PT boats had arrived at Mariveles and were waiting to take the nurses off the peninsula. Denny stayed with the bus, as Taylor and Reider carried bags and other belongings down to the pier and pitched them over to the crew members. As the powerful motors churned into the quiet sea, Helen Summers managed a faint smile and waved good-by to the three men standing silently on the pier. When the boat was out of sight, they returned to Little Baguio and joined the preparations for surrender sure to take place the following day.

The bugles fell silent across Bataan.

4.

Death March

The general order went out for all commanders to raise the white flag. At 10 a.m., the Japanese advance troops, walking carefully behind a tank, reached Little Baguio. A gunner on top of the huge vehicle menacingly poised two 50-caliber machine guns, ready to answer any last-minute resistance.

Taylor stood beside Colonel Schwartz, chief hospital surgeon. Together they managed a final salute as two enemy soldiers lowered the American flag. Once on the ground, it was unceremoniously stamped on and mutilated.

A few minutes later the full Japanese battalion approached the hospital entrance. They were led by a well-trained interpreter who spoke perfect English. He wore hobnailed shoes with forked toes made from carefully processed pigskin. He had a black stringy beard and wore clean, patched gray green breeches and leggings. A tiny cap, with long flaps down the back, protected his neck from mosquitoes and the sun. To Taylor, he looked confident and cocky.

Colonel Schwartz escorted six Japanese prisoners out to meet the column then surrendered the hospital to a Japanese lieutenant who had been waiting in the tank.

The officer in charge screamed an order to the interpreter. "All Amerikajin and Hiripin soldyars assemble in front of hospital!" Guards were dispatched to the main entrance of the makeshift building, apparently to keep the wounded from being harmed by the cadre. But there was no protection for the thin line of officers and men who, at the captors' command, formed at the front of the hospital.

The soldiers began stripping their arms of watches, taking rings from their fingers and pilfering all other personal belongings.

At first Taylor could not remove his ring from his swollen, callused finger, but finally, he sucked his finger furiously until the ring came loose. He took a final look at the Baylor University crest and handed it to the guard.

By midafternoon, Bataan had settled into a state of complete abeyance. Guns ceased firing. Troops discontinued their movements. Smoke and dust cleared away from the jungles. Birds began to chirp again.

The faces of the defeated Americans were tense. For weeks the stubborn defenders had refused repeated demands to surrender. They felt strong that the battle had not been lost to the Japanese hordes but to disease, lack of medicines and starvation. Nevertheless, they had accomplished their mission as a sacrificial holding force. They had stopped the Japanese shock troops' southward plunge toward Australia. To capture the island bastion, the high command in Tokyo had been forced to bring in troops from Malaya, China, the East Indies, and even the homeland.

The interpreter approached Colonel Schwartz and told him all personnel who could walk were being moved to Mariveles. Only the doctors would remain to care for the bed-ridden patients. Taylor joined the ragged column and marched from Little Baguio to the East Road, where they were forced into trucks and driven to Mariveles on the tip of the peninsula.

Mariveles was in a state of bedlam. The major force of 68,000 Filipinos and 12,000 American soldiers had already arrived. They sat docilely in large groups on the dirty runways of an old airfield that had been used as an emergency landing strip by American pilots during the battle for Bataan. Mountains surrounded the area, with a central plain running east to sea level. It was the hottest point on Bataan. Near the black volcanic-ash beach stood an old lighthouse where ships' crews were once inspected before receiving permission to enter Manila Bay. Naked Filipino babies and dogs watched curiously from the doors of the huts.

Taylor had heard a legend about the little barrio. A priest had fallen love with a young Filipina named Maria Vales, but because of his vows he couldn't marry her. Her family moved from the city to the plain. The priest followed and built the first church there, near Maria.

Now chaos and complete lack of organization added to the tragic situation. Japanese intelligence had calculated that there would be 20,000 prisoners instead of the 80,000 they captured. In addition, there were twenty-six thousand Filipino civilians who had fled the cities in the wake of the Japanese onslaught.

Frantic guards tried to form the prisoners into groups of 300, only to yield to frustration as thousands milled round them. They vented their feelings by slapping and kicking those who did not instantly obey their orders, which were all given in Japanese. Taylor jumped out the back of the truck and joined the milling masses of men. They were haggard shadows of once proud soldiers, now in bloodied, tattered rags. As he observed the frantic guards he felt a strange premonition – the years ahead would be molded into a caste of death at the hands of cruel taskmasters.

The sun dropped behind Mount Mariveles, bringing a cooling reprieve to the men standing in the blistering heat Long gray shadows, ghostlike invaders of the serene, green mountains, stretched lazily over the plain teeming with the bitter, disenchanted men. Some lay on leaves, others on the bare ground. All were silent. Any sound – a cracking leaf, rattling mess kit, or helmet falling against a stone – might bring a burst of fire from the machine guns set up at 50-yard intervals. Throughout the night intermittent bursts could be heard, immediately followed by screams. Then all was silent again.

At first light, the Japanese continued separating the prisoners into groups of 300 They formed two columns – prisoners of war on the left, civilians on the right, with guards strutting up and down the middle. The first contingent of prisoners stretched clear across the ruins of the little barrio.

Throughout the morning, Taylor watched dozens of tank commanders and hundreds of cavalrymen as they futilely attempted to organize the march. He observed group after group as they passed by. The boy from Texas, a company commander from Iowa, and others trudged past. Some he recognized, others he had never seen before.

Another contingent stopped in front of where he sat. The guard began ordering the prisoners to their feet, kicking and beating those who were slow to respond. Taylor jumped to his feet and began helping some of the weaker men. Another soldier also broke rank and assisted.

"Down but not out, eh, Preston?" Shocked, he turned and saw Father Duffey. His voice sounded like an angel's; he looked like the devil.

"Never out, Duff," he answered, glancing cautiously toward the guards. "Never out." They helped the remaining men to their feet, returned to the long scraggly line and waited again.

Duffey, a squat little man, rested on his haunches and looked up at Taylor. He was barefooted and his breeches were torn. His knapsack was covered with mud. His heavy black beard was matted.

Taylor looked down at the little chaplain, squinted his eyes and said, "If your bishop catches you without your robes, he'll excommunicate you."

"I'm not communicatin' anyway," Duffey quipped. "If he saw me now, he'd vomit, I stink so bad."

The men standing nearby laughed, the first encouraging sign Taylor had seen since he arrived in the middle of the pandemonium. They stopped abruptly when a Japanese guard charged toward them yelling, "you no raugh. We teach you no raugh."

By noon it had been twenty-four hours since the men had received food or water. Suffering from heat exhaustion, they began falling like flies. Their buddies tried to pick them up, but sometimes they fell, too. Any man who could not stand on his feet was promptly bayoneted.

It was quickly apparent the Japanese had no intention of following either The Hague or the Geneva Conventions governing POWs. The guards were carrying out the Emperor's will and believed no guilt would be attached to attacks on American prisoners. In that distorted mirror they saw themselves as patriots fighting an American imperialist conspiracy to conquer their homeland.

Rumor ran rampant through the ranks. It spoke of a prisoner exchange, trucks waiting to move them north, and of General Wainwright's capacity to hold Correg-idor indefinitely. None seemed plausible to Taylor. There was nothing to exchange for the POWs, and there weren't enough trucks in all the Philippines to move that many men. And the old nemeses – starvation, sick-ness, and lack of supplies – would soon overwhelm Wainwright. It was inevitable.

Another story told of the missionary family of five who walked down from the mountains waving a white flag. A Japanese Zero spotted them and, with one ma-chine-gun blast, killed the whole family – father, moth-er, little boy of five, little girls of four and three. The in-cident was supposed to have occurred three days be-fore, just outside Mariveles. The burly sergeant who re-lated the story had helped bury the children. He said one little girl was still clutching a rag doll.

At 1 p.m. a Japanese officer stood on a knoll jutting into Manila Bay north of Mariveles. He waved a huge yellow flag signaling the beginning of the march. An in-terpreter over a loudspeaker yelled, "Americang and Hiripin soldyars taku hwat carry. Marchu."

Guards were stationed every twenty or thirty feet. One guard glared menacingly at the cross Father Duffey wore around his neck. Maneuvering the point of his bayonet dangerously close to the protruding Adams's apple of the chaplain's neck, the guard cut the chain, flinging the crucifix into the dust that was already four inches deep along the trail. Father Duffey later nick-named him "The Shadow," since he couldn't escape his narrow, beady eyes. Seldom did he take his eyes off the chaplain. Taylor warned his friend to take every precau-tion and obey every rule.

The column trudged north out of Mariveles toward the mountain road leading up from the plain toward

Little Baguio, and as the ragged line stretched across the plain toward the mountains, it reminded Taylor of a medieval funeral procession with thousands of mourners. But in contrast to mourners, they felt unsure of their destination, and some knew they would never survive.

Dust clouds, stirred up by the continual procession of trucks and marching men, swirled so thick Taylor could barely see. His eyes burned, his throat choked. He tore off part of the leg from his breeches and made a mask. It helped very little.

As troop convoys passed by, soldiers jeered at the prisoners and all the time "The Shadow" continued to dog Father Duffey's steps. Any time the priest fell behind or stumbled, the guard hit him with the butt of his rifle. Already his face was bruised and bleeding. Dust caked on his wounds looked like dried mud tinged in crimson.

Taylor purposely walked behind Duffey. Each time the little chaplain lagged behind he put his arm around Taylor's shoulder and received a brief reprieve from the sun and dust.

Immediately behind Taylor walked a private from Nevada. Everyone called him Tex, although no one knew why. He was tall and gangly. He had been racked by dysentery for days. At times he lapsed into delirium. Taylor tried to talk to him to help occupy his mind. Sometimes he would answer, but often he only looked straight ahead.

Two hours out of Mariveles, Tex threw away the bundle he carried. A few steps later he stumbled and fell into the dust. Taylor stopped, placed his body between the fallen man and the approaching guard, and waited to bear the consequence. Slowly he lifted the boy to his feet. Another soldier joined him. His arms clinging tightly around the necks of the two comrades, Tex continued down the road.

The road curved, crossed a wide river and began its descent through the foothills toward the Zigzag. Taylor saw hulls of American ships and the destroyed dry-docks in the bay near the beach. The whole area cracked with preparations for artillery emplacements, being made ready for the final assault on Corregidor, the last outpost of democracy in the Far East. Bulldozers cleared away littered weapons and burned-out tanks. Japanese planes, keeping constant surveillance on the march, flew back and forth over the lines, buzzing, dipping their wings to their own troops.

All along the road abandoned packs, helmets, blankets, and canteens littered the ditches. The further they marched, the more the castoffs increased.

Tex, unable to perspire because of lack of salt, was in agony. Fever would drive him into delirium, then chills would rack his body.

Taylor stopped, called a guard, and said, "This man is sick. He needs water and medicine."

"So sori, so sori, you marchu!" he answered. He grabbed Tex by the collar, pulling him out of Taylor's hands, then threateningly pointed his bayonet, he ordered him to continue in the line.

"Korosuzo!" he said, threatening to kill Taylor. For a brief moment the chaplain hesitated. As the guard cocked his rifle, two other marchers grabbed Taylor and forced him back into line. After a few paces he heard the other prisoners gasp. Looking back, he saw the guard wiping blood from his bayonet, then kick Tex's headless body into the ditch.

The mountain road rose from the sea like a giant pyramid robed in all shades of green. Rocks loomed from the side. Two boulders high over the peak were nature's lookout over the dreadful procession. Another angry-looking rock formation jutted out over the bay. Huge macopa trees, some 80 feet high, dotted the valley to the left. Stately maniknik trees, giant patriarchs of the forest, stood silent over the tragic scene.

The ascent up the mountain became more treacherous with each step. The guards' eyes darted from prisoner to prisoner, ready to pounce upon and dispose of any who fell. Taylor realized that human endurance alone could not see him through the ordeal. He whispered a word of encouragement to Duffey, who appeared to be on the verge of collapse. The words were like a tonic to the priest, and his short, faltering steps suddenly became firmer.

Occasionally they would pass a naked corpse, the face swollen and covered with maggots. The body, stiff and already beginning to blacken in the intense heat, was already covered with flies, and carrion birds tore at the flesh.

To amuse himself, a guard pushed two prisoners, kneeling with hands raised in supplication, over the side of a cliff. Their screams ended only when they hit the jagged rocks below.

The Filipinos fared no better. Because they had fought side by side with the Americans, they were brutalized all the more. To add to the indecency, the guards would pull the young girls from the ranks, drag them into jungle and abuse them repeatedly. Then they allowed them to rejoin their families. Anyone who resisted was shot. Frightened mothers rubbed human dung on their daughters' beautiful faces to make them unattractive to the guards.

Conditions continued to deteriorate. The sickening

smells of accumulated excreta, combined with the
stench of decaying bodies, defied Taylor's own imagi-
nation. He realized that if something was not done, the
march would turn into the most awesome blood bath
the world had ever known. Apparently they were not
regarded as prisoners of war but as criminals. Their
only crime: defeat in battle. No relief appeared. The
guards allowed no rest.

As the road curved to the right, Taylor glanced back
into the valley. He could see Mariveles in the distance.
The miles of road between were lined with marching
men.

Unexpectedly, the guards again yelled, "Speedo!
Speedo!" Taylor's contingent had fallen behind. The
guards began trotting at double time up the steep slope.
Men dropped everywhere and were quickly bayoneted.
Anyone who tried to help them was shot. All semblance
of order disappeared. The prisoners stumbled over their
own comrades.

Filipino women and children, suffering from starvation, dysentery, and exhaustion, fell to the ground.
Many marchers, semi-delirious with fever and thirsty,
saw mirages – the old swimming hole, mountains of ice,
barrels of Coca-Cola. One prisoner said he saw the
garden hose spraying water over the lawn in the yard
back home.

A gray-haired World War I veteran stopped, unable
to move further. He ripped open his shirt and bared his
chest for the guards, begging for death. They pulled a
curly headed kid from the ranks and handed him a
club, ordering him to beat the old soldier. The boy refused. They held a pistol to his temple and pulled back
the hammer. The boy raised the club, closed his eyes
and struck. There was a thud, and the older man

dropped to the dust, dead. The march continued, but the boy later lost his mind and never recovered.

Taylor saw that Father Duffey was growing weaker with each step. Moving up beside him he said, "It'll soon be night, duff. Then they'll let us rest."

"Preston, if I drop . . . if I drop, the last rites . . . you'll say them, won't you?"

"Don't think about it, Duff. Think of night and rest."

"The Shadow" moved over beside them and screamed, "Damare zo!" Taylor knew it meant to shut up. He did.

Night settled slowly over the mountain road. But still they marched. The blistering sun had disappeared, but the gnawing hunger and searing thirst remained. Then another tormentor, the devilish malaria-carrying mosquito, began to inflict its punishment on their exposed bodies.

Along the side of the road they could hear cooling springs of water rushing to the valley below. Taylor saw a prisoner break rank and dart toward the water, hiding in the entanglement. A guard mechanically lobbed a hand grenade into the underbrush. Following the cacophony of the ear-splitting concussion, the trail was silent again.

Marchers began stumbling over the corpses of prisoners who had fallen in the road.

Few of the living had the energy to pull them to the side; the guards didn't bother. Even bodies that couldn't be seen could be smelled. The stench made Taylor want to vomit, but all he could do was retch and gag.

Taylor noticed he was less hungry, but the tormenting thirst remained. Trancelike, he would imagine he saw water before him only to jolt back to reality just before falling down.

His feet burned and his legs ached. He tried to massage the muscles above his knees but was unable to knead the clammy, greasy skin. Cramps throbbed through his muscles, but he dared not stop.

During the night some of the POWs, suffering from cerebral malaria, went insane. Some extended their arms in pleading gestures and trembled. Some would salute an imaginary flag. The attacks usually lasted about thirty minutes.

The solemn cadence of dragging feet beat out a weird rhythm as the shadowy force moved through the Philippine night. The weaker prisoners had already fallen. For a while the guards concerned themselves with their own tired bodies rather than amusing themselves by inflicting pain on their captives.

At 5 a.m. the sun, a blazing ball of fire, returned. The prisoners neared the summit of the mountain.

"We made it, Duff!" Taylor squeezed his friend's arm, but unable to speak, the priest answered only with a faint smile.

Filipino civilians lined the road at the top of the Zigzag. Some handed canteens of water and cans of milk to the prisoners. Others were beaten back by the guards. Little children, holding papaya, bananas and stalks of sugar cane, waited until the guards passed, then quickly handed the food to the starving prisoners.

An elderly Filipino woman handed a cup of water to Father Duffey. His eyes sparkled as he raised the cup to his parched lips, but "The Shadow" hit him in the mouth with the rifle butt, and the tin cup cut into his mouth. Blood and teeth fell to the ground. He dropped to his knees, folding his hands in prayer. The enraged guard ran his bayonet through his side, then placing his foot on the fallen man's throbbing body, pulled the blade from the flesh.

Taylor knelt down and held his friend's head in his cupped hands. "The Shadow" stood close by, a look of relief on his face, as though able to relax now that his personal vendetta was completed.

Taylor, wondering if he too would be stabbed, prayed silently. "Lord, have mercy on your servant. He's a good man who served you well. Receive his soul." As he held the gasping body, the guard ordered him back into the line. When he looked back, he saw some Filipino civilians drag the priest, still breathing, into the jungle.

Several hundred men had passed by, silent witnesses to the execution. None knew Father Duffey was a chaplain. His bayoneting was only another episode of the nightmare from which they could not awaken.

"Close friend, huh?" The voice sounded sympathetic and kind. "I'm Shurtz."

Taylor extended his hand and returned, "Taylor, Preston Taylor." Yes, he thought, a real friend.

Shurtz, a major in an old cavalry unit, was tall with thinning sandy hair. He had survived the night better than most of the prisoners. Even so, the strain was etched indelibly on his boyish face.

Taylor had never felt such excruciating heat. Although the climb up the Zigzag had been an Augean task, there had been a cooling ocean breeze and occasional shade from the sun. Now all the cover was stripped away. The breeze had vanished. He took a dirty rag from his hip pocket and pressed it down over his blistered ears for protection.

Waves of heat, like the silent vanguard of an invisible army, rose from the road. Chalky dust clung to Taylor's sweating body.

Big caterpillar tractors towed 250-millimeter siege guns toward the bay as preparations continued for the attack on Corregidor. Ammunition trucks followed the creaking vehicles, grinding into the dust the bodies of the dead along the road. Taylor tried to pull a body from in front of the clamoring tracks, but he was pulled back into line by Shurtz just before a guard, his gun at level position, fired.

"Don't fight it, Taylor. Your time will come. Not now," the major counseled. Taylor pondered his words briefly, then dropped his head and prayed for forgiveness for the hatred he felt for his captors.

Avoiding strands of barbed wire and stepping over the stiff forms of fallen captives, the men moved on down the road. A Filipino boy, no more than thirteen, fell and dropped to sleep in the muddy ditch beside the road. A guard whacked him repeatedly on the buttocks until he awakened and jumped back into line. An American airman, naked from the waist up, ran to a stagnant pool of muddy water to immerse his head in the cooling liquid. A guard, swinging a bamboo club, ran up behind him yelling, "Mizu, nai! Mizu, nai!"forbidding him to drink even the filthy liquid disguised as water. He hit the airman behind the neck, knocking his head under the water. As the man struggled to rise, the guard hit him again. The third time he just lay face down in the water, dead.

Taylor's mind began having periods of complete blackout as sunstroke wrestled for control of his senses. When he regained his senses, he tried to concentrate on names, dates, cities, countries – anything that would occupy his mind. He counted the days of the month, the months of the year, then repeated them in reverse. He tried to remember the forty-eight states and their capitals. Birthdays of the members of his family were hardest to recall. Then he envisioned Ione, his wife. Where was she? What was she doing? All the time he wondered if she would be thinking of him. That was important. What if she thought he had died?

Coconut trees lined the shallow, muddy river emptying into the ocean 200 yards away. Taylor gazed at the large acacia trees. He knew they had stood long before the prisoners and captors were born and would still stand after they had died. Elephant-ear leaves on the banana trees swayed gently back and forth. Patola flowers, a beautiful yellow with intense green vines, spread underneath. The scene reminded Taylor that love was as strong as hate, and life longer than death.

Tall cogon grass, with its stately white tassels, flanked the line of march as the column slowly drifted toward Cabcaben.

When they arrived at the outskirts of the little barrio, Taylor noticed a villa on the right side of the road. It was the House of Castillo, where General Wainwright would surrender to General Homma a few days later.

A Filipino boy standing beside the road raised his hand in a victory sign and said, "Hi Joe!" smiling through a mouthful of rotted teeth. A guard grabbed him by the collar, pulling him into the tall grass, where he beat him into unconsciousness.

Taylor discovered he no longer could assimilate all the treachery into his reason. All the tragedies – and the thought of further possibilities – made him yearn to destroy his own identify, run away, escape into the world of the unnamed, where everyone was no one. But there was no place to hide. His soul was becoming like a burnt log, last survivor of a great conflagration, smoldering, spent. A thousand hot embers jabbed at and seared his nerves. Hate, the archenemy of the God he professed to serve, caused his face to flush in indignation. His whole world was haywire. Yet personal recovery seemed nowhere in sight.

Tantalizing thirst, oblivious to his spiritual dilemma, antagonistic to his deeper feelings, swayed and molded his thoughts. Only as he prayed could he refrain from cursing the day he was born. Only as he remembered the beauty of the past and his love for Ione could he find courage to walk even one step further into the ugly future.

Beheaded bodies could be seen in the ditches all along the bomb-pocked road as the worn-out men with expressionless faces aimlessly shuffled down the road. Only the brave stole glances at the open sepulchers lining either side.

Suddenly a private, marching a few paces behind Taylor, fell into a ditch. A burly Japanese officer, his saber clanking against his brown leather boots, rushed over to the soldier and kicked him in the groin. Two guards lifted the man up as the officer beat him with his fists. Unexpectedly, the soldier regained consciousness, gritted his teeth, and spat in the officer's face.

"Korosuzo!" the officer yelled, condemning the young boy to death.

The line of march stopped. The guards tied the man's hands behind him and knocked him to his knees. The officer removed his razor-sharp sword from its scabbard and raised it into the air. For an instant the whole world hesitated. Then, with a swift blow, the officer severed the man's head from his body. The dust turned to crimson mud.

"They've gone crazy." Major Shurtz shook his head as the columns passed on through the jungle." Crazy."

Ominous rain clouds floated across the peninsula from the east. Taylor's consciousness faded, and faintness threatened his survival. He looked longingly at the clouds. In them he saw spectators cheering in the coliseum as armed gladiators made sport of helpless, defenseless combatants.

"Lions fourteen, Christians nothing!" he yelled. No one near him seemed to notice. Then lukewarm drops of rain splashing off his forehead brought him back.

Bluish smoke rose in spurts from the bahays in the next little barrio. Civilians lined the road and shouted greetings to the ragged army. It bolstered their morale, their only remaining possession. The Japanese officers, hoping to parade the prisoners through the street in exhibition, were angered by the rousing welcome the POWs received from the Filipinos. In retaliation, they ordered the people back from the road, but the crowds refused to move. They continued cheering and throwing food to the marchers.

Taylor caught a piece of panocha, hardened sugar cane, and began sucking the sweet stalk. It was his first food in three days. Then he broke the piece of cane and handed half of it to Shurtz. It wasn't much, but it saved their lives temporarily.

An hour later, guards ran up and down the columns shouting, "Tomare! Tomare!" They led the prisoners off the road and down a trail to a rice paddy once used by the wallowing carabao. Some of the prisoners saw a puddle of water with a covering of green scum, and several recklessly cupped their hands and drank until they were contented. None knew it was polluted with dysentery amoeba, nor would they have cared. Taylor and Major Shurtz made a pact to keep one another from drinking the infected water no matter how thirsty they became. They vowed to restrain one another – by force if necessary.

About a hundred feet from the paddy the Japanese had piled mountains of canned goods. Major Shurtz walked across the paddy toward the sentry guarding the food. "Takusan food. You give, okay?" he pleaded, pointing to the stacks of boxes.

"Dai jobu, hokay," the guard replied, as though complying to the major's request. Instead, he swerved and cracked him on the head with the butt of his rifle. A huge knot rose on the side of the major's head and blood trickled down his neck.

Men standing near the edge of the paddy began digging for cincomas, little vegetables left over from the harvest. After brushing away the dirt, they took a bite and passed the remainder to another man.

The guards crowded more POWs into the paddy area. They strung barbed wire around the perimeter to discourage escapes during the night. After ordering the prisoners to sit down, the guards relaxed.

Taylor tried to talk to the man next to him. Words, one by one, syllable by wretched syllable, had to be torn out of his throat. Finally he stopped. The man, a slightly built sailor, didn't seem interested anyway.

A bald-headed captain, his overseas cap resting precariously on the back of his head, said, "The worst scene in the world this is. What's God like to damn men to the likes of this? We're dead already. All's left is the funeral. We won't even get that."

"Oh, is God to blame?" Taylor asked painfully. "Does he guard the food, hoard the medicine, wield the sword?"

"What you taking' God's side for?

"I believe He wants to help us."

"Then why doesn't he wipe out the Nips?"

"Force just isn't his way."

Suspicion flushed the captain's face. Pointing toward the sky, he said frantically, "If God were up there, he'd get us the hell out of this hellhole."

Noting the man becoming bitter, Taylor changed the subject. "My name's Taylor, Preston Taylor, chaplain."

"Oh? Well, that figures, I guess," the man said, his voice trembling but calmer than before. "Excuse me, Chaplain, I just lost my head."

Taylor cut his words short. "Forget it, Captain."

Somewhere in the mass of huddled men, a Filipino became delirious and began to scream. After thrashing around on the ground he went into spasms, then dropped into a coma. He awakened a few minutes later and began raving in Tagalog, his native tongue.

The stench of human waste lingered over the whole area. Although the men were exhausted, few could rest.

Beyond the captain sat a twenty-year-old corporal, his head covered by a bloody bandage made from strips of army blanket. During one of the numerous shakedowns a Japanese guard had discovered he possessed some yen, the Japanese currency. Believing he had taken it from a dead Japanese soldier, the guard had grabbed a bolo and cut off the corporal's fingers.

About midnight, the black clouds belched torrential rain. The downpour, common in the tropics, caused those already trembling with malaria to chill and pitch. One by one they slowly began lowering their heads, at last finding relief from life, begun in innocence, ended in cruelty.

The rain stopped as suddenly as it had begun. A few

minutes later, a rumor spread through the enclosure that guards were bayoneting all prisoners. The men began to stampede, and those too sick to move were trampled to death. They stopped only after the guards had fired point-blank into the hysterical mass, killing a large number of prisoners.

When morning came, the captives were moved out of the paddy. The "buzzard squad" remained behind to kill the prisoners who couldn't walk.

After marching several hundred yards down the road, the guards suddenly forced them off the highway toward the beach. They threw lugao, rice mush, at the captives. Each man was supposed to receive three table-spoonfuls, but most of it fell to the ground, and the men scratched animal-like in the sand for just a morsel. The inadequate water ration only served to increase their thirst.

The order to continue the march was delayed. As usual, the Japanese overseers were in a state of confusion. To amuse themselves, they assembled a group of twenty officers, tied their hands behind them and, after removing their shoes, watches and shirts, gave them the "sun treatment." Taylor and Major Shurtz were among the hapless victims forced to kneel with their faces exposed to the burning sun.

Flashes of heat exhaustion attacked Taylor's mind. He tried his old game of concentration again. Although they had captured his body, he vowed no man would enslave his soul. Concentration took him back to his seminary classes – ethics, theology, preaching, evangelism. Arbitrarily, he set up a silent dialogue, pretending to repeat the oral exams, the final phase of the long journey toward his earned doctor's degree. It worked. By the time he had successfully completed the series on ethics and prepared to enter theology, he felt a guard untying his hands.

When they were untied, seven men, including Taylor and Shurtz, walked away. The others had succumbed to the three hours of torture.

The signal to march was finally given, and the prisoners moved back onto the road. Their ranks had been greatly decimated during the night. Although Taylor had seen nearly eight hundred bodies during the two days, he guessed the worst was yet to come. And as the skeleton army moved slowly up the gravel road, hot volcanic cinders felt like live coals on his bare feet.

As the heat increased, Taylor's sensibilities decreased. The ornamental vines of the brilliant purple bougainvillea flowers changed into patterns of a kaleidoscopic variety of crystals. The greenish brown trunks of the towering Philippine oaks formed beautiful hues of patina. Rock-riddled mountains became crenelated fortresses; pine trees, their dazzling defenders.

Taylor returned from the world of fantasy all too quickly. He caught himself yearning for the heat to play more tricks on him, releasing him, if only temporarily, from that caravan of the condemned, blackened stumps and scorched earth.

Major Shurtz walked like a dumb mannequin. Only his legs, rotating monotonously like a wooden soldier's, differentiated him from a walking corpse. Occasionally Taylor would see his lips quiver as he mumbled a few words. Then his pace would quicken as though he had been the recipient of some added stamina.

Visions of death crept into his thoughts. "Dying is not so bad," he soliloquized. "But dying like this. In the valley of the shadow of death, God is my God. Without him, what would it be like?"

A voice seemed to reply, "Not death, but life. Think of life. You'll live."

"I'll live! Taylor shouted. "I'll live!"

When he regained his senses, Major Shurtz was holding his shoulders, shaking him violently. A curious guard ambled toward them. Taylor steadied himself for the expected kick, but instead of hitting him, the guard removed his canteen from his belt and handed it to Taylor. Unsure of the intent behind the apparent act of kindness, Taylor hesitated. Then, still unbelieving, he raised the canteen to his lips and took several swallows. Then he handed it to the major, who drank and passed it on down the line. Once more, they had sidestepped the mark of death.

"Why did he do it?" Shurtz asked after taking his turn at the canteen. There's no rhyme or reason."

Taylor wasn't fully convinced it was the Japanese guard, but maybe a divine messenger. Stranger things had happened. Anyway, he felt strangely inoculated against death. He was convinced he would live.

To break the humdrum repetition of dragging feet, the captors concocted bizarre recreation. Using Filipinos as human pawns, they played a game of chess until one of them became bored and delivered the ultimate checkmate.

The Filipinos meekly bowed to each grotesque vagary. Once a guard spotted an extra-large coconut in a pinnate-leaved palm and ordered a small popeyed Filipino soldier to get it. His slight hesitation was met by three bayonets, threatening to pin him to the trunk of the tree. Quickly he shinnied up the trunk, grabbed the fibrous husk, and threw it to the ground. Immediately the guard split it open with his bayonet and began to eat the tender meat.

Back on the ground the little Filipino stooped to pick up the husks, still containing a little meat. The guard, a devilish grin on his face, rammed his bayonet through the man's neck pinning him to the ground.

A comrade, unable to bear the horrible specter, broke rank and ran to aid the dying soldier, but the other guards intercepted him with their rifle butts, knocking him unconscious. Bent on stamping out any shred of rebellion, they pulled three other Filipinos from the column, handed them shovels and ordered them to dig. When the hole was completed they ordered both injured men, one with a mortal neck wound, the other still faint from repeated blows on the head, thrown into the open grave. Then they motioned the gravediggers to begin covering them. The men refused, but, prodded by a cocked pistol held behind their ears, they began turning the dirt.

Soft clods falling on their face startled the addled man. When he realized what was happening, he went berserk, and the guard, as though waiting for an excuse, plunged his bayonet into the screaming man's chest.

At Limay, the prisoners were herded into an old corral that had been used as a stable by Japanese cavalrymen. Two guards, holding long bamboo clubs, flanked the entrance. The slightest provocation cost a prisoner a swift kick in the abdomen or a blow across the back. It was a bitter introduction to the corral that already reeked with the acrid, corrosive smell of animal excreta.

A Japanese cavalryman, watering his horse near the pen, saw the wishful eyes of a prisoner standing close to the bamboo fence. He handed the bucket to the POW, who emptied its contents while the guard watched and laughed.

The guards threw nigiri, rice balls, into the corral. But most of them fell to the filthy ground. Taylor managed to get a small handful and gave it to a young airman named Bill. Three times Bill tried to swallow the rice, but each time he vomited it back up. After each attempt, he developed hiccups that caused his whole body to retch.

Major Shurtz tapped Taylor on the shoulder and said, "Preston, look! Ambulances!"

Taylor craned his neck to get a better view of six American field ambulances with dingy red crosses still visible on the sides. Their drivers were Japanese, but an American officer was in the lead vehicle.

After speaking briefly to the officers in the command tent, the American, accompanied by two guards and an officer, headed toward the corral.

To Taylor's astonishment, it was Colonel Schwartz, the hospital commander. The colonel approached the pen, glanced at the prisoners briefly, and angrily demanded food and water. The Japanese officer returned to the tent and a few minutes later reappeared with several guards carrying buckets of water and boxes of nigiri. The colonel supervised the distribution.

After each man had received a small portion of rice and ample water, Colonel Schwartz turned a bucket upside down and stepped up on top of it. "Men, I want all the worst cases brought out and put in the ambulances."

The men who were still able to walk gently lifted their friends out of the filth and carried them toward the waiting ambulances. While the Japanese guards turned their faces to avoid the stench.

Scanning the pale faces, the colonel asked if there

were any doctors. There was no reply.

Then the colonel spotted Taylor. "Chaplain, is it you?"

Taylor didn't answer, only stood in disbelief at the sight of someone actively engaged in patching up the remains of the worn-out men.

"I want that man," Schwartz said, pointing to Taylor.

"Go, Preach, and God go with you," Shurtz said, smiling.

Solemnly Taylor said good-by to the major and several others standing nearby. Then he reached down and picked up Bill and carried him toward the gate.

"Colonel, this man's mind is gone. He ought to go with the other patients."

"Okay. Put him in the ambulance. You're going with me, Taylor. The men at Little Baguio need you.

Taylor laid Bill on a litter in the back of the ambulance, then returned to the cab and got in beside Schwartz. The convoy moved out south toward Little Baguio.

Along the sides of the road lines of prisoners stretched as far as the eye could see. The dead, both American and Filipinos, lay in the ditches beside the road.

Bit by bit, Schwartz shared the remarkable story of how he had received his freedom of movement. During the battle for Bataan, twenty six wounded Japanese prisoners, including a colonel, had been brought to the hospital for treatment. When a Japanese general had learned his men were receiving the same treatment as the Americans, he issued orders that the hospital was to be left alone and allowed Schwartz to keep the ambulances and pick up the wounded along the highway. As a result, Little Baguio had nearly three thousand patients.

The ambulances met a column of tanks that forced them off the road until they passed. Dust, churned up by the grinding tank tracks, was as thick as fog. The tankers, wearing thick goggles, stared suspiciously at the two Americans in the lead ambulance. The wounded men in the back coughed as though they would hack their lungs out.

When the last tank passed, they moved on down the road.

"Glad we found you, Preston. You'll have a lot of work to do at the hospital."

Taylor was glad, too, but already he missed the major and the others. He looked out the window at the columns of men as they continued the death march. He wondered what would become of them. Would they survive? Would he see them again?

"I'll do my best, Doc. I'm thankful for the chance."

"Your friend, Bill Dawson is there and Reider. They've been working around the clock," the colonel said.

The convoy covered the distance from Limay to Little Baguio in an hour. It had taken a day and a half by foot. The sentries posted at the entrance waved them past.

Captain Reider stood at the main door of the bamboo building. When he spied Taylor a look of disbelief swept over his face. Then, trying to smile, he quipped, "About time you came back to work. Taken any bus rides lately with pretty nurses?"

"Heard you were about to go under. Thought I better come bail you out."

After chatting for a few minutes, Reider returned to

the operating room, and Taylor joined the orderlies removing the wounded men from the ambulances, but he had caught Reider's expression. Something had shocked him. A few minutes later he caught sight of himself in a mirror and immediately understood Reider's reaction. He didn't recognize his own face. It was scabby and burnt. His long beard was matted with every kind of filth. His swollen eyes had become narrow slits. He ran his fingers across his cracked bleeding lips.

Taylor saw Bill being lifted out of the ambulance and carried to the psychiatric ward. The boy saw him too, but his face remained expressionless.

As the last man was carried into the hospital, Taylor saw Chaplain Dawson running toward him. He stopped a few paces away and stared in disbelief. Big tears welled up in the corner of his eyes. Then he ran toward Taylor and threw his arms around him. Taylor didn't speak. Seeing Bill Dawson, his close seminary confidant, was more than he could bear. With his arms clinging tightly around the man's neck, he cried unashamedly. Talking in spurts, interrupted only by laughter, they walked to a row of tents beside the hospital. In front of the tents stood a fifty-gallon barrel filled with water.

"That's the shower, Preston," Dawson said, as he handed him a straight razor and a bar of soap.

As the cool water dripped down his face and the soap cut away the putrid smells, Taylor's mind wandered back to the death march. He wondered what they were doing – the major and all the rest. For a moment he caught himself wishing he were back with them.

Then praying silently, he said, "God, you brought me here for a purpose. Help me to be up to it."

Not only did he look like a different man, he felt like one. Following a supper of fried bananas and lugao, prepared by the Filipino cook, he accompanied Dawson on a tour of the wards. Everywhere there was evidence of repeated bombings.

Taylor noticed that most of the patients were American. They were lying on litters, straw mats, and some just on leaves. They had every wound imaginable, bodies mangled, limbs torn. Some were blind. Other suffered from shell shock. Occasionally he saw Filipinos. They always smiled.

The demented men in the psychiatric ward touched Taylor's heart most. They had lost all control of the relationship between body and mind, and they babbled unintelligibly. Dr. Reider was assigned to the ward, and Taylor asked for permission to work with him.

The next morning, just after daylight, Taylor and Dawson visited the wards where twelve hundred ambulatory patients and more than eight hundred other wounded men were being treated. They divided the twenty wards into sections of ten. Each chaplain could visit nearly two hundred men per day, seeing each man once every five days.

Taylor walked briskly down the narrow rows of beds and litters. Some of the patients still slept. Others stared blankly at the inside of the crude cogon-grass roof. He noticed blankets over the faces of two men who had died during the night. The burial detail, busy around the clock, would probably move them out before noon.

"Aren't you the chaplain from McKinley?" a voice asked.

"Yes, I'm Chaplain Taylor." He searched the faces of

a half-dozen men lying side by side on a pile of leaves.

"I'm Red Coolidge. I was with the Second Battalion at McKinley. Use to go hear you." His voice was barely audible as he spoke through worn-out bandages, greenish-brown from Unguentine, that wrapped completely around his face. There were two holes for his eyes and a narrow slit for his mouth. On his shoulders irregular-shaped nodules, full of water, bore mute witness to a nasty burn. His brows and lashes had been burned away. His eyes were so matted with pus he could hardly keep them open.

"When were you brought in, Red?" Taylor asked, taking a rag from his pocket, dampening it in water, and wiping the boy's eyes.

"Yesterday. They picked me up near Bagac on the West Road."

"You're lucky to be alive."

"Yeah. My whole outfit caught it. We were holed up in a big nipa house. Had white flags everywhere. Jap troops passed the hut and yelled something to us. We were getting ready to go out when they hit us with flame throwers. Guess I'm the only one left."

Beside Red, a big Negro boy, hearing voices, began to rouse.

"What's your name, son?" Taylor asked.

"Charley, sir. Just call me Charley." He tried to sit up, but slumped down. The chaplain carefully placed one hand behind his neck, another under his back, and gently lifted him to a sitting position. Blood was still draining from a crusty bandage around his stomach.

The other men were wide-awake. Their eyes, distant and cold, scrutinized Taylor. Carefully they weighed each inflection of his voice.

Charley's eyes flashed wishfully as Taylor took a

New Testament from his shirt pocket and searched for a specific passage. Without introduction he began to read.

"Come unto me, all ye that labour and
are heavy laden, and I will give you rest.
Take my yoke upon you, and learn of me;
for I am meek and lowly in heart; and
ye shall find rest unto your souls."

Charley stared pensively at the ceiling. Slowly he began to sing, "What a friend we have in Jesus, all our sins and griefs to bear ..." Voices throughout the ward joined in the song. The hellish hole of death seemed suddenly transformed into a peaceful place of worship. Men, their faces hardened by pain and despair, sang lustily the words of hope.

A Japanese guard poked his head through the ward door to see what was happening, then walked sleepily away.

Taylor's heart was a little lighter as he left the ward. He knew the men had found something that could never be purchased with money, nor taken away by sickness and privation.

Early the next morning a truck convoy pulled up to the hospital storage area and began loading supplies. Colonel Schwartz protested to Lieutenant Kaneko, the officer in charge, that these were fruit juices and meats kept in reserve for the critical patients, but Kaneko only glared at him.

Patients in the wards, overhearing the colonel's protests, lined the sides of the building and watched as the last of the food and medical supplies were loaded into the trucks and hauled away.

Colonel Schwartz was boiling. He shook his fist in the lieutenant's face, and two guards raised their rifles. Kaneko signaled them back, and Colonel Schwartz retreated, knowing it would be impossible to recover the supplies.

At 7 a.m. the next day the vibration of Japanese 250s shook the ground. The hospital walls rocked back and forth, and dust filtered down through the nipa roof onto the patients, making them cough. American batteries on the Rock of Corregidor returned the fire, and cheers swept through the hospital as the big guns pounded the enemy. But hope was short-lived. Cheers turned to panic as shells began falling near the hospital, rooting up trees and digging deep craters in the moss-covered jungle floor.

Ward 14 took a direct hit. As Taylor ran toward the burning debris, he could hear men screaming. Dr. Reider was there trying to restore calm, aiding the worst injuries, but the helpless patients continued to scream.

Taylor entered the south door just at the ward was hit again. He dove into a drainage ditch at the hospital entrance and was immediately covered by limbs, dirt and flying debris. Slowly he began squirming out from under the wreckage.

When the smoke cleared away, he was greeted by more tragedy. The shell had hit directly beside where Red and Charley had been. No trace remained.

Captain Reider had miraculously survived, although his clothes were rags. He held a man, already dead, in his arms. Mangled bodies were strewn all through the wreckage. Pieces of human flesh protruded from the bamboo walls. The scent of burning flesh was everywhere.

Horror-stricken patients began to flee the buildings.

Guards picked the stronger ones and used them as human shields as the big American guns rained death on the hospital.

Reider and Taylor feverishly removed burned men from the rubble and then hurriedly made their way through the cowering men toward an isolation area where the battle-fatigue patients were quartered. Colonel Schwartz and two orderlies were frantically trying to control the three hundred and seventy men, some of whom were trying to kill themselves.

In the corner, a gray-haired patient began to babble. An officer, brandishing a piece of broken glass, tried to kill Reider. An orderly disarmed him, but not before he had slashed his own throat. The colonel stared at him in disbelief, then ripped off his shirt and tried to bandage the neck wound, but it was too late. In a few minutes the man was dead.

Taylor sat down beside the man, put his face between his knees and wept. Around him, some of the shell-shocked patients imitated barking dogs, recited the pledge to the flag and laughed inanely. Others, dressed only in their underwear, wandered aimlessly through the ruins.

Then, as quickly as it had begun, the battle ended, and quiet settled once again over the hospital. Many of the guards had run into the jungle when the duel began. Now one by one they returned. Lieutenant Kaneko ordered all prisoners who could walk to begin digging a single, narrow trench behind the hospital to bury the dead. It was dark when the trench was completed. Two hundred and seven men, mostly naked, were dropped into the open grave. Taylor, his hands covered with blood, approached Lieutenant Kaneko and asked permission to conduct a burial service.

"Dame, zo," the lieutenant bellowed, turning him down. He barked another order, and the guards began forcing the diggers to cover the bodies.

The personal amnesty under which Colonel Schwartz had so freely worked was being stripped away. Water, flowing plentifully in a stream nearby, was rationed. All food was taken away. Sentries, nettled by the threat of a second artillery engagement, screamed at the prisoners. The slightest breach of conduct earned a rifle butt in the face or a clubbing with a bamboo stick.

Day after day the shelling continued until only one ward remained standing. The colonel placed the most critical cases inside, the others outside, exposed to the sun by day, prey for mosquitoes by night. Following each barrage, the burial detail continued digging.

And General Wainwright, cut off from all supply lines, finally ran out of ammunition. The firing pins on the big guns were thrown into the sea. The indomitable Rock had fallen.

A few days later, truckloads of prisoners from Corregidor began passing along the road near the hospital. Occasionally they stopped to take on water. Bit by bit, by talking to the men, Taylor pieced together the events surrounding the final defense of Corregidor.

During the initial drumfire the Japanese artillery had lobbed sixteen thousand rounds on the American positions in twenty-four hours. Dive bombers had become so accurate they were hitting the gate at the mouth of Malinta Tunnel. When the water supply ran low the general feared for the lives of the patients in the thousand-bed hospital inside the tunnel. He raised the white flag.

A radioman told Taylor of Wainwright's final message to President Roosevelt: "Please say to the nation that my troops and I have accomplished all that is humanly possible. May God bless you and guide you and the nation. With continued pride in my gallant troops, I go to meet the Japanese commander. Good-by, Mr. President."

A few days later, Lieutenant Kaneko informed the colonel that trucks were being dispatched from Manila to pick up the remaining hospital patients. Schwartz, skeptical of Japanese promises, warned the men that it could be just a rumor, but when the announcement was made, their faces lit up with hope.

The next day at precisely 10 a.m. a convoy of old Benz trucks arrived. It took four hours to load the patients, since the guards refused to help. Then Lieutenant Kaneko ordered that all the unconscious patients, about seventy men, be left behind, and when Schwartz protested, he was placed under guard in the lead Benz.

At 2 a.m. the trucks pulled away from the shambles that had once served as a busy hospital. Only the "buzzard squad" stayed behind to take care of the unconscious prisoners. None were ever heard from again.

5.

BILIBID

It took two hours to cover the 65 miles from Little Baguio to Manila. The trucks slowed as they approached the fortress of Bilibid, then drove through the forbidding gate of the old Spanish prison near the Intramuros.

The prison fortress had been built during the Spanish occupation. Death cells where Filipino patriots had been executed were still being used. The walls were twenty feet high and four feet thick, made of native stone from the mountains around Baguio. Six evil-looking strands of barbed wire were attached to vertical wooden poles placed at seven-foot intervals.

In the center of the compound stood a nondescript, three-story building with a corrugated steel roof. Rain towers extended from three gables. Taylor thought the towers had a striking resemblance to pictures he had seen of helmets worn by Genghis Khan's Mongol soldiers.

The outer walls covered a city block. Another wall, with four steel gates, bisected the compound in the middle.

Lieutenant Kaneko led the men to the wall, turned a key in the heavy gate and slowly opened it. As Taylor stepped through he saw a row of cells that looked like cages on the left. In front there were eight narrow bars from left to right welded to eight vertical ones. The side and back walls were solid concrete. Each cell housed four men stretched out on dingy mattresses. Some read, others lay idle.

Just ahead he saw an open hole in the side of another thick wall. The lieutenant led them through the wall down a spiral staircase into the damp, musty dungeon. A small electric light bulb provided the only light.

Taylor reeled back as he saw an unconscious prisoner, a large muscular man, dangling from ropes tied to his thumbs. A long hall ran through the shadowy dungeon, dividing the cells. Opening the doors, the guards pushed the prisoners inside, four to a cell.

The heavy door slammed, and the key turned the lock. Had it been the closing gates of hell, it could have sounded to worse to Taylor. In the dim light filtering through a small opening at the top of the door he could barely examine the cell. Four mattresses lay along the side, and on three of them he was just able to discern dark, lifeless forms like cumbersome sacks of rice. He placed his little bundle on the empty mattress and sat down.

The smell of human excreta nauseated him. A rat appeared from a cavity in the floor, paused and then ran unafraid across the face of one of the sleeping men, who awoke, flailing the air wildly. He sat straight up on the mattress and, seeing Taylor, was momentarily startled.

"Oh! Just got here, eh?"

"Five minutes ago."

"That's long enough in this place. We call it the bottomless pit, Aboddon, the place of the lost. Me, I'm Jones."

"The guard we call Apollyon," another voice said. "I'm Arty. The sleeper is Big Joe."

Clasping their clammy hands, he replied, "I'm

Taylor."

"Can't say I'm glad to see you," Jones said.

Slapping the big man on the leg, he said, "Wake up, Joe. We got a guest come for dinner."

As though drugged, Joe groggily awakened from his stupor and tried to focus on the new cell mate.

"Yeah, okay. Tonight's menu is a little rice, a little water, water-lily green," the big man said.

"In Bilibid we have death, hunger and disease – otherwise no problems," Jones added.

"Where did the Nips snare you?" Arty asked.

"Little Baguio at the hospital."

"All Bilibid is a hospital, without wards, without doctors, and without medicine."

Piece by piece the puzzle surrounding Bilibid began to fit together. They were fed once a day unless some infraction of the rules by a prisoner caused the infuriated commandant to withhold food from all the prisoners. Every three days they were let out of the cells for a walk in the yard. The man hanging by his thumbs at the entrance to the dungeon was being punished for splitting open a guard's head. They called him Rial and said he was a pilot.

"It started over the women," Jones explained.

When twenty army nurses were brought in from Corregidor, Rial saw a guard try to drag one up to a sentry box and hit him on the back of the head with his fist. They had let the girl go, but Rial has been hanging there for two days.

"Beats solitary," Big Joe put in. "No lights, lots of crackups."

Taylor wondered if the girls could be the same nurses he and Reider had hauled to Mariveles, and if

Hattie Brantley or Helen Summers had been in the group.

Later he learned that Bilibid was a clearinghouse for various prison camps and work details throughout the island. Rebellious prisoners were sent to Fort Santiago for torture. The healthy were sent to the mines, road details, or to work on the docks. The rest were indiscriminately incarcerated in the two giant prison camps – O'Donnell near Tarlac, and Cabanatuan at the terminus of the Manila railroad at the Sierra Madre mountain range.

Abruptly, the conversation ended. The three men went back to sleep, and Taylor labored to bring a semblance of order out of the chaotic ruins of his surroundings. He couldn't sleep like the other men, who apparently had become accustomed to the roaches, tumblebugs and rats that ran freely under their feet.

A maggot climbed awkwardly to the top of his mattress. Taking careful aim, he flicked it with his middle finger, sending it to the back wall with a thud. The cockroaches were wilier, more alert.

The next day the prisoners were lined up in the yard. They stood at attention as the men from solitary, still in manacles, dragged by and left for Fort Santiago. Across the yard the army nurses appeared, led only by a bowlegged guard. The troops whistled and howled; the nurses waved back. The guards acted embarrassed. Taylor recognized none of them.

Big Joe was pulled out of the ranks and assigned to a work detail headed for Mindanao. Arty and Jones were placed with the group going to O'Donnell. But Taylor was ordered to Cabanatuan Prison, a giant detention complex six miles east of the city of Cabanatuan. His morale soared when Chaplain Dawson was singled out of another group and ordered to the same camp."

6.

CABANATUAN

The air felt free and clean outside Bilibid, the sky seemed a little brighter. Taylor's pace quickened as he followed the guard out of the prison area toward Dewey Boulevard, which parallels the bay for several miles and then continues on to the railroad station.

Hundreds of waiting prisoners milled around the giant terminal. As usual, everything was in a solid state of confusion. The Japanese had miscalculated the number of trains necessary to transport the prisoners to the various prison camps and the prisoners, sitting on the six long station platforms, waited impatiently.

As Taylor looked at the men, he realized they were becoming less than men, less than they once were – or should be. They were hungry, diseased, cowed – a tattered remnant of a once-proud army.

The guards compensated for the lack of trains by creating a shuttle routine, round-trip routings from Cabanatuan, barring common breakdowns, taking about four hours.

It was past midnight when an apish colonel ordered Taylor's group of about thirty men to begin loading into the boxcars.

The old train, previously used to transport cavalry horses, was humid and dirty. The reek stunned Taylor as he climbed up a makeshift stair step into the stifling heat of the car.

It will hold about forty, Taylor thought, surveying

the car, undersized by American standards. But the guards pushed and shoved ninety-nine men, all bound for Cabanatuan, into the car, then bolted the rusty door.

With the door shut, air no longer circulated. Humidity – maximal at Philippine midnight – compounded the discomfort. Men gasped for air. Animal dung covering the floor burned their bare feet, and yet, Taylor noticed, the men accepted the situation almost philosophically and without complaint.

A boy next to him fainted, laid his head on Taylor's shoulder and remained standing because it was too crowded for him to fall.

Two hours later, when the train entered Cabanatuan station, half of the men in the car had lost consciousness. Two were dead.

Those who could jumped out of the door into the fresh night air. Taylor and Dawson carried an unconscious boy to a little patch of grass beside the platform. He awakened briefly, tried to move his lips, and then died with a look of terror on his face.

Could a man's soul shrivel, decay, rot like the body? Taylor wondered. Could the spiritual flesh wither away, leaving only a skeletal framework, devoid of strength, resistance shattered, and hope in eclipse?

Dawson began saying a few words over the boy.

"You said it, Lord. When we walk through the valley, you'd walk with us. That's all we have left. We claim it for this boy."

He paused for a moment, realizing he didn't know the boy's name.

"You know him, Lord, and his. A mother worrying about him, praying every night. A wife standing alone, waiting for some word. Children lonely for their daddy."

Fighting back the burning tears, Dawson tried to continue the prayer, but Taylor touched his shoulder. "He'll be okay now, Bill. Let's move him."

They carried the body to the back of the station where twenty other bodies, victims carried from all the boxcars, were lined up in a single row awaiting burial. After laying it gently at the end of the row of motionless corpses, Taylor looked into the starry heavens and said, "Master, we commit them to your mercy. We know nothing else to do."

For the remainder of the night they bivouacked near the cockpit behind the station, where Filipinos once gathered each week for chicken fights. The next morning they would make the six-mile march to the Cabanatuan prison compound.

Taylor was miserable. Unable to sleep, unable to stay awake, he dozed, and then was awakened by a rifle shot. He was relieved to see the reddened sky, announcing the new day.

At daybreak the troops were ordered to move through Cabanatuan into the country. As they entered the Bangad Valley, Taylor saw the Sierra Madre Mountains rising out of the distant plain like a gray-walled citadel. The flat land on either side of the road was sectioned into patterned rice paddies. Being in the country raised the captives' morale. The quiet, beautiful countryside gave temporary relief from themselves, their tortured minds, diseased bodies, and gnawing hunger.

As they walked through the barrio Cabu and on across the dusty, shadeless plain, they met a small band of Negritoes, slight aborigines from the mountains. The women, smoking black cigarettes, carried baskets on their heads. The little black men bartered their wares, mainly fruit, vegetables and tobacco, with the Japanese guards.

The Negritoes, simple dawn people fresh from the rugged mountainous outback, giggled as they lowered the baskets from their heads and carefully placed the wares on the ground. Taylor glanced at the contents – bananas, mangoes, nuts of various kinds, and a few balls of rice.

One of the Negrito women, less than four feet tall, her thick, curly hair cropped close, flashed a smile toward the prisoners and offered them a stalk of bananas.

"Oi, dame yo!" the guard yelled, refusing permission for the act of kindness. Then he walked over to the woman, handed her a few pesos and took the entire basket.

At 10 a.m. the detail turned right off the main road and marched the remaining three hundred yards to the camp entrance. The guards herded them into the main parade ground for their first briefing by Captain Tanaka, commander of the POW camp.

As the captain harangued through an interpreter, Taylor's eyes wandered over the surroundings. He noticed the sides of the buildings were bare, the skeleton bamboo frameworks exposed. Cogon grass roofs dropped to the ground. A dozen or more barracks, some with concrete foundations, lined the back wall of the massive enclosure. They seemed to be about fifteen by twenty-five feet. He judged the complete compound to be about one hundred fifty acres. The camp, he remembered, had originally been constructed as a training center for the Philippine Scouts. Now all the bamboo thickets and underbrush had been cleared from the perimeter of the camp so that the guards in the watch tower could see anyone attempting to escape. White-plumed cogon grass, looking slightly like a sea of waving flowers, formed a backdrop for the compound.

A little road in the southeast section ran in front of the barracks, turning abruptly as it joined another one going directly south.

The other prisoners, all Americans, stared curiously at the new arrivals. Taylor noticed that most of them stood inside the barracks or milled around the parade ground. There were no Filipinos, and he learned later none were allowed inside the camp under penalty of death.

The commandant, gesticulating excitedly, his fingers punching hole in the fetid air, continued the "pep talk."

Taylor discovered he could count the prisoners' protruding ribs at a glance. Puppets on strings, he thought, more dead than alive, their faces introducing old men where young men ought to be.

After thirty minutes the commandant ended his tirade. The interpreter bowed politely three times and continued to bob up and down from the hips as the officer, his spit-polished brown boots sparkling in the bright sun, stepped off the platform.

Taylor craned his neck and watched the little puffs of dust following the commandant's footsteps across the yard. Then he turned and saw a lone figure, an American officer, approaching from the opposite direction. Unceremoniously, he mounted the platform, bowed stiffly to the interpreter, and announced that he was Colonel Gillespie, ranking officer in Cabanatuan.

"Can't say I'm glad you're here, but you are, so we'll all make the best of it. Basic administration is left up to us. We have more than five thousand men here, and it keeps growing every day. Each man is assigned to a group of ten. If one escapes, the guards shoot the other nine. Simple as that. We muster each morning at seven.

When you fall out, form at the entrance to Barracks Number One for barracks assignments."

He squinted, hastily scanning the ranks of the new men.

"Any questions?"

"Yeah, Colonel, when do we eat?"

A registration desk for barracks assignments had been set up in front of the barracks called number One. Taylor and Dawson joined in the long line. A sleepy-eyed American sergeant asked the men for their name, rank and serial number and condition of health. His face had a green cast, revealing a recent bout with malaria.

"Taylor, Chaplain Captain, 0-384411, health good as can be expected."

After a few more minutes, the sergeant sent a clerk across the yard to another building, and soon Colonel Oliver, who had been chief of the twenty-six American chaplains assigned to the Philippine command, walked briskly to the desk.

Colonel Oliver greeted them warmly, smiling at their surprise, for they had not expected to see the old man again. He told them Morris Day and Zerphas had arrived in camp a few days earlier. Taylor's heart beat faster when he heard Morris Day's name. He didn't know Zerphas, but Day had been his closest friend, except possibly Bill Dawson, in seminary, and he was eager to see him again. When Dawson asked the colonel about the other chaplains, he sadly told them that twelve had been killed on Bataan. Some of the survivors had been sent to O'Donnell. Through bits of information gleaned from other prisoners, the colonel had learned that Smiley had died on Bataan, Parker had been caught in a bombing raid prior to leaving Manila, and Keller, Raines, Spivak and Ellsworth had died on the march. The rest were missing.

"Duffey didn't make it, sir." Taylor paused briefly then explained how the beloved Catholic chaplain had died.

Oliver, a trusting man, couldn't believe it had all happened and was still happening.

"If we eat tonight, we'll meet with Zerphas and Day."

The implication in his voice troubled Taylor. He interpreted it two ways: They may not eat, and if they didn't, they might not have enough energy to get together. He didn't like the sound of it.

"I'm assigning you to the hospital," Oliver told him. "Zerphas and Day have the barracks, and I've tried to work the wards. There are thirty-one, you know. Always full."

The sergeant told the new arrivals they would bunk in barracks Number Eight, and Colonel Oliver took them there, telling them to grab a bunk and then report to the superintendent's office, where he would introduce them to Colonel Gregg.

The bunks were bamboo platforms about a foot off the floor, twenty-six inches wide. The chaplains spread the blankets, which were loosely folded at each end of the bunks, over the knotty bamboo structures that served as both springs and mattresses.

A man, lying on a nearby bunk, advised them to hide their things.

"If the Japs don't get it, the thieves will," he said.

"We'll leave it," Dawson answered. "There's nothing the Japs could want, and if our men need it worse than we do, they can have it."

In the superintendent's office Colonel Oliver introduced them to Doctor Gregg, who welcomed them by
saying, "I'd like to offer you a chair, but chairs aren't on
the basic-necessity list issued by the Japs – nor is medicine, equipment or bandages."

Carefully, the doctor studied the two young faces.
His expression changed into something bordering on
pathos, then changed again as he said jokingly, "Some
place for a pack of preachers to wind up – the butt hole
of creation."

"Preachers have been in some tough places before,"
Taylor answered. "The fiery furnace, the lion's den, on a
Roman cross. We'll be all right."

Taken somewhat aback, the doctor fumbled through
a stack of papers, and then said bluntly, "I'll square
with you. We're whipped, medically speaking. We're
using knives and saws for operations and amputations.
We've reached the end. There's very little we can do for
anyone now. There are thirty-one wards in this complex, and each handles a hundred men. We're already
to capacity, but more sick and wounded are coming
into Cabanatuan in droves every day. There are more
patients in the hospital than there are troops in the
yard."

"Tell us what to do, Colonel. We'll begin right now,"
Dawson said.

"First, I'll show you the wards," Gregg said. He rose
and started for the door. The two young chaplains and
Colonel Oliver followed close on his heels.

7.

The Hospital

Dr. Gregg led them through a row of rooms cluttered with litters, worn-out equipment and operating tables gloomy with rusty probes, tarnished forceps, scissors and saws, down a corridor into Ward One. It was obvious that there were too many sick and wounded for the small core of medical workers to handle. Patients bathed in sweat lay on rough litters. The whole area reeked with the nauseating smells of blood, stale sweat and diluted remains of what had once been chloroform. Bluebottle flies swarmed through the room and landed on open wounds.

Kneeling beside a litter, Taylor saw a soldier's leg half-rotted away with gangrene. The boy was unconscious, but periodically his whole body jerked violently. The doctor said the guards had brought him in that morning and went on to explain that the whole jungle was crawling with anaerobic bacteria, and that anything exposed to this bacteria became gangrenous. Since the supply of serum was nearly exhausted, the doctors left the wounds open to the sun and air in hopes of its healing.

A doctor carrying a roll of lint stepped out of the operating room. His name was North, a tall, pleasant man who smiled and shook hands vigorously when he was introduced to the chaplains. He took over from Gregg and led them along a loosely covered ambulatory portico to the various wards, explaining how their toughest enemy was gastrointestinal illness that caused dysentery in every conceivable form, showing them the mass of POWs suffering from malnutrition, their hair thinning and sometimes changing color, introducing them to the blind patients suffering from lack of Vitamin A, and finally winding up in Ward 31.

"This is Zero Ward. Some call it 'The Pearly Gates Ward.' Guess you men know more about that than I do. I'll excuse myself now and get back to work."

He left them, and the three chaplains returned to Colonel Oliver's barracks. As they walked through the doorway, Morris Day bounded off a bunk and hugged his two former seminary classmates warmly. Then he introduced them to "Zerph" Zerphas, a dark man with an extending nose that crooked a little to the left at its end. His heavy black eyebrows gave him the appearance of a bear, but a genuine warmth and a depth of kindness radiated through all the tapestry.

For a few minutes they talked animatedly. Then Colonel Oliver interrupted to say, "Men, I want to pray and thank God for the confidence he has placed in us by letting us be in this place at this time."

The five men dropped to their knees around the bunk and remained silent for several minutes. Then the colonel began to pray:

"Lord, we cannot see tomorrow, but you hold all our tomorrows in your hand. We dare not question why you've led us here; only help us give a good account of all we've learned of you. And if . . . and if you should ask us to pay the supreme sacrifice, as you were once called upon to do, let it be with confidence that you will meet us at the river and lead us across the troubled waters. We claim this same support for all our men here, some even now at the point of departure. In Jesus' name, Amen."

The men continued in silent prayer for another twenty minutes; then, when all had finished, Oliver began the assignments. Zerphas and Day were to work in the barracks, with Day also helping Oliver in the yard. Taylor and Dawson were to have the hospital, and by mutual agreement, each was to work with the cases he most wanted – Taylor in Zero Ward, Dawson with the blind.

The meeting broke up and Taylor stepped out onto the parade ground. Men were returning to the barracks from work details near the river, doing minor assignments for the Japanese, or just milling around the yard. Others stood in line at the one spigot which supplied water for the entire camp – already swelled to six thousand men. The line was always long, Taylor was told, and sometimes it took several hours to get a drink, depending on the disposition of the guard, who might, without provocation, turn it off, announcing no more water that day.

A shrill bugle blew three sharp blasts, signaling supper, and Taylor saw lines already forming in front of the large steel caldrons placed in several locations around the parade ground. Behind each caldron two cooks were serving food.

"Yeah, yeah, Whistle wood Soup," Taylor heard a black soldier just in front of him chant as he thumped the bottom of a metal utensil fashioned from a discarded can that once contained sixteen ounces of Campbell's pork and beans. "Yeah, yeah, Whistlewood Soup."

Behind the black man several other prisoners, their eyes wild with starvation, edged closer and closer to the caldron filled with a steaming, purple liquid.

The whole camp stirred with new rhythms as one by one they received a cup and a half of the rice-gruel soup made of scraps from the rice-house floor. It had turned purple, as always, when cooked. A few water lilies floated on top.

Following his first encounter with "Whistle wood Soup," Taylor returned to the barracks to meet the older chaplain.

At the end of the drab, dimly lit building, he saw two prisoners meticulously constructing a bed of some old pieces of wood that they tied with rattan strings. They placed layers of cardboard over bamboo rods for a mattress, then stood back and proudly stared at their creation. Their satisfaction was short-lived. A guard charged through the door and kicked down the bed, scattering the various pieces.

"Baka zo!" They got the message. They had heard baka fefore. But they didn't like being called fools now any more than the first time they had heard the word. Slowly, almost mechanically, the prisoners cowed away. The guard, muttering curses to himself, stamped out of the barracks.

Taylor listened intently as Colonel Oliver briefed the men on the critical situation.

"The camp commander forbids all gatherings, even for worship."

"For how long?" Dawson asked.

"He didn't say, but if he thinks it will add salt to our wounds, it'll be indefinite. He's a real sadist."

"Yeah, Chaplain Oliver and Colonel Gillespie go to see him every day, but he always says the request is being considered by higher authorities," Zerphas said.

"Temporarily we'll hold secret meetings, just quoting a Scripture, offering a prayer. It'll keep us hopping, but worship and precious little faith is all that's left in this place," the colonel said.

"Colonel, the burial detail, the last rites, what goes?" Taylor asked.

"Up to this point they have withheld any permission for conducting funerals. We lost seventy men yesterday, and Doctor North says Pearly Gates is filling up fast tonight."

"Preston, we're hamstrung," Morris Day added. "They won't even let us sing hymns in the wards."

From somewhere outside a bugle sounded taps.

"Lights out," Oliver said.

"Tomorrow night, Colonel?" Day asked.

"We'll see. Tomorrow, go directly to your posts and do what you can." He paused, raised his hand gently, and added, "And God go with you, boys."

Day and Zerphas picked their way through the milling men toward the rear entrance and entered the adjoining barracks. Taylor followed Dawson out into the moist, hot night and headed toward barracks Number Eight.

"What do you make of it, Preston?" Dawson asked.

"It's bad – worse than bad, impossible," he replied, but inside he refused to accept the impossibility. God, he thought, had made a mockery of lots of impossibilities. He may do it again.

Exactly at 9 p.m. Cabanatuan completely blacked out except for the coal-oil lamps in the guard hut and the omnipresent tower lights zigzagging in and out of the shadowy compound.

The sudden darkness signaled the mosquitoes to emerge, and Taylor wrapped the blanket completely around his body for protection from the droning hordes. Nevertheless, they got to him through the open ends, and his battle for peace lasted seemingly endless hours. At last, though, he was able to drop off to sleep.

At sunup, he rose and crossed to an open hole in the barracks wall that had been originally intended for a window. Across the parade ground he saw a squad of guards raise their flag, then turn toward the sun and bow stiffly three times.

"Wake up, Bill,' he said, and soon the two men were on their way to the hospital, where Colonel Gregg met them at the entrance.

There were several other men, volunteers for the burial detail, led by a good-natured sergeant who had only one upper-front tooth intact.

"Colonel, we're uh - "

"Speak up, Sergeant," the colonel barked.

"Well, we want a doctor to go to Pearly Gates with us. Uh, we're afraid."

The sergeant's dark eyes looked directly at the colonel's and saw a flush of anger sending red streaks up the side of his neck and into his face.

"Afraid? Afraid?"

"Not like that, Colonel. The other day we laid one out and were getting ready to cover him up, you see, and, well, I looked down and he was still breathing, and, well . . ."

"I see, yeah, okay. I'll send a doctor in each morning."

Taylor followed the detail to the death house. The squad's dragging feet beat a solemn cadence on the dirt floor as they went to the end of a row of hospital buildings to the last ward, the death house, set off from the others near the open latrine.

"Sergeant, I'm Chaplain Taylor."

"Hi, Chaplain."

"All volunteers?"

"Yeah, but we're getting fewer and fewer each day."

"Oh?"

"No soap," he added, looking down at his callused hands. "We can't wash our hands after it's over. It bothers the younger ones, the smell and all. Yeah, the dead flesh just clings to your hands and it bothers the younger ones."

"And you?"

"Guess I never thought much about it. It's no picnic, but these men can't help themselves any longer." And he stepped into the Pearly Gates Ward, the charnel house of lost and forgotten men.

One by one the squad carried the dead men through the doors and placed them on litters. Taylor counted sixty-eight. Another twelve were unconscious and probably wouldn't make it through the day.

Taylor felt completely helpless. He ached to pray over the men and give them a Christian burial. He had thought his mind had been prepared for anything. Apparently, it wasn't.

It took about an hour to clear the ward. Round trip to and from the camp cemetery, 1600 feet to the north, took roughly eleven minutes. It was the longest funeral procession Taylor had ever seen, moving out of the main camp area to the graveyard, then circling and beginning again.

He walked over to the sergeant. "Sergeant, I'm joining the burial detail."

"But sir, you're an officer, and the enlisted men have been assigned the graves."

"Maybe so, but I'm going with you."

"But sir, the trench – well, it's pretty rough work. We grub it out with homemade hoes."

"Okay, I'll grub with you."

The men paused, dumbfounded as Taylor reached down and grabbed the front end of a litter. The sergeant picked up the back, and they walked toward the cemetery.

He soon learned that the sergeant's description of the common grave didn't tell half the story. Although the trench was to be only three feet deep, most of the dirt had to be removed by hand or placed in buckets and lifted out.

The dead soldiers were carefully placed side by side in the grave. Just before they poured the first clods of dirt over their lifeless bodies, Taylor glanced toward the guards, who managed to keep a noncommittal distance, fearful they would pick up some disease from the dead bodies.

Certain they would not notice, Taylor slipped down beside the grave and fell on his knees, folded his hands under his chin and reverently bowed his head.

"Start grubbing tomorrow's trench," the sergeant ordered, winking at the men and stealing a glance at the guards about a hundred and fifty feet away.

Taylor's parched lips opened and he began to pray.

"God, the whole world is on trial here. They showed no mercy on these men. But we plead for your mercy. Receive their souls into your kingdom, take away their pain, wipe the tears from their eyes. Some have wives, Lord, and sisters and brothers and little children who are waiting for them, but who will never see them again, maybe never know how they died. Comfort them and spread your great arms of love about them. Into your hands we commit these good men. May the cause for which they died never be in vain. In Jesus' name, Amen."

Without regular worship services, there was little hope of bringing out the spiritual and emotional aspects of the men's personalities and thus develop added strength. Although they continued to read the Scriptures and conduct brief devotions for small groups, the chaplains always labored under the commandant's prohibition of any kind of religious ceremonies.

One day, Taylor spotted a young soldier reading the New Testament.

"What passage are you reading?"

"Oh, none in particular. Just scanning some stories."

"What's your name, soldier?"

"Mike, Chaplain."

"Where you from, Mike?"

"Texas."

"Oh, I'm from Texas, too."

As the chaplain drew closer, he saw that the boy was paralyzed from the waist down. He also had trouble turning the pages. The doctors had told Taylor about the boy and his fight for life, but his condition was seriously complicated by dysentery, and life was ebbing from him.

"Texas is great, ain't it, Chaplain."

"Mike, I wouldn't trade a spoonful of Texas for a carload of anywhere else."

The young boy's dark eyes sparkled and a faint grin crossed his face.

"Yeah, wouldn't it be something to see those dust devils spinning across the flats? Sometimes I see and smell, almost taste, that place. But those days are gone forever."

The chaplain silently prayed for wisdom to comfort the young trooper. Then, cautiously, he continued: "Sometimes all we have left is our hope, and that's one thing nobody can take away from us."

Mike was silent a minute and then replied: "Yeah Chaplain, I've always wanted to have hope in something. Now that the end is near, it is even more important, but it's all so hard to understand. It says here, 'The Lord is my shepherd.' But I've always figured he's the Japs' shepherd, too, and leaves a hell of a lot of confused sheep."

The young soldier paused and then continued: "When this first happened to me I said, just wait till I get my hands on whoever's running this cockeyed world. But reading the Psalms and the Gospels has shown me just how wrong I've been."

"Mike have you ever thought about turning your life completely over to Christ and accepting him as your Lord?"

"I've thought a lot about it these past few days, especially after the doctor was honest enough to tell me I only have a short time left."

"Would you like to do it now?"

"Yeah, but nobody has ever told me how."

This was almost more than the chaplain could bear. For weeks he and the other chaplains had been in and out of the ward, yet no one had taken time to speak personally with the boy about his spiritual need. Suddenly he could hardly hold back the tears.

"It's okay, Chaplain, I didn't mean to say anything."

"It's not that, Mike. It's just that God wants you to trust him personally, and no one has ever explained to you how you could do it. But I'd like to help you right now."

"Sure, Chaplain."

"It's like this, Mike. God created all the people on this earth but it was an unusual creation. For instance, he made us free. He wanted us to love him, but he wouldn't force us to do so. And man took his freedom and strayed away, very far away, from God."

The young man listened intently as Taylor continued: "So God decided to do something else to help man. He actually visited this planet in order to live with the people he had created, and ultimately to die for their sins. You know who that was? It was Jesus Christ."

Taylor glanced to the south end of the barracks and saw a guard stick his head inside the door, then slowly walk away.

"But after he died, he arose from the grave, thus showing his power over death. And if he could do that himself, it means he can do it for us when we die. But the secret is for us to fully trust and believe what he has done for us, then apply it to ourselves."

"But how?" the boy asked.

"In prayer, Mike. We pray and ask him to forgive us for anything we've ever done that displeased him, and then tell him personally that we want to receive his as our Savior. At that point, he comes into our life in a new way, and we're never the same again. Would you like to do that, Mike?"

"Well, I would if it weren't for . . ."

"For what, Mike?"

"I know I'm going to die," the boy said softly, "and I'm afraid that my wanting to straighten things out with God is because I know I'm going to die, and it just don't seem right. I never was interested in God before."

The chaplain, sensing a time of decision was at hand, prayed again for spiritual guidance to help the boy. Then, as if in direct answer to prayer, he remembered a story from the New Testament.

"Sure, mike, and I think I understand," Taylor said.

"But God is not man and he doesn't think like we do, nor is his response to our need based on the timing of our actions, but on his great love for us.

"Jesus himself one day told a story that might help you understand it better. It was the story of the workers in the vineyard. Would you like to hear it?"

"Sure," Mike replied.

"Well, a farmer early one morning hired some men to work in his vineyard and agreed to pay them a regular wage, a silver coin a day."

And Taylor told him the parable of the workers in the vineyard.

"Well, I guess God is sorta like that," Mike said when Taylor concluded the story, and after a moment both he and the young boy bowed their heads in prayer.

Slowly, the chaplain prayed that the boy might have a full understanding of the decision he was about to make, and then invited the boy to pray.

"Well, Lord, I guess this is the first time I ever prayed, but I've thought about it lots, and now want to ask you to help me." He hesitated briefly, then continued: "You know I haven't always done what you wanted and I'm sorry, cause it would have been better if I had. But I want to be right with you and now trust you as my Lord."

For several minutes neither spoke. Even those patients lying nearby seemed particularly quiet, and for a few fleeting moments the dirty, smelly hospital ward was turned into a holy place as the young trooper called on God.

"May the Lord bless you, Mike, and he'll keep you forever and ever," Taylor said.

"Sure, Chaplain, I believe it," he replied." "But there's one thing more. After it happens, you know, when I'm gone, I want you to write my wife, Anna, and tell her things weren't so bad. We have a little girl named Mary Kay. She's two now. I ain't never seen her, but my wife sent me a picture and all that. Just tell her it wasn't so bad."

The young trooper, his hand trembling, reached up and took his dog tags, and with a jerk broke the thin chain and handed them to Taylor. As he placed them in the chaplain's hand, he squeezed it gently and a wide smile crept over his face.

Two weeks later the boy died. It was several days before Taylor felt able to write is widow and little Mary Kay, but it had to be done, so he went to a little hut near the center guard tower – a place jokingly called "The Library" – and sat down on one of the bamboo stools scattered around a rectangular bamboo table. He took a piece of the soiled, brown Japanese paper from the center of the table, and after a moment of reflection, began to write:

Dear Anna and Mary Kay,

It is my unhappy task to write that your husband and daddy died last week in the hospital in Cabanatuan.

About two weeks before he died, he asked me to do him a favor – to write you and say he loved you and that everything was all right, even to the very end.

During those last days he found a very close relationship to the Lord. His New Testament and times of prayer became very important to him, and the genuine religious encounter which he experienced was an inspiration to all who knew him.

His body lies in the camp cemetery just south of the compound. A handmade cross marks his grave. Perhaps, when the war is ended, his remains will be sent back to Texas. I know you would want it that way.

And little Mary Kay, your daddy was a real hero. He served his country like the real man he was, and always remember that you will be able to live in freedom because your daddy died.

He loved both of you and his last thoughts were of you.

Perhaps when this war is ended, I will be able to visit you. God bless you both.

Sincerely,

Capt. Robert Preston Taylor
Chaplain, 31st Infantry

8.

SHADOW OF DEATH

Troops from throughout the Philippines – mostly sick and wounded – continued to pour into Cabanatuan. From mid-April to the following December, more than 8000 prisoners were crowded into the compound. During that time, 2500 died from sickness, maltreatment and starvation.

Although the death rate was high in Cabanatuan, transfer prisoners reported circumstances in other prison camps bordering on outright genocide. In Camp O'Donnell, during the first nine months of incarceration, more than 40,000 American and Filipino prisoners died. The grapevine said the chaplains in O'Donnell, who had more freedom of movement, conducted as many as 500 funerals per day.

Most men endured the months of ever-present death throughout the camp without hysteria or fear. As they approached the door of death, they maintained a calm and trusting composure.

Taylor discussed the phenomenon often with the other chaplains. "There's only one explanation," Taylor said to Bill Dawson one day. "The men were raised under the teachings of Christ, and even though some were less faithful than others, they trusted the Supreme Being and hoped for the best after death."

"That faith prepared a man not only to live but also to die," Dawson replied. Somehow the troops had learned to expect the worst. And if anything better came along, like survival, they were joyfully surprised.

Dying was easy for the prisoners, but living was hell. The Japanese guards saw to that. They worked overtime contriving methods of punishment.

Late one afternoon, Taylor witnessed a group of men being punished for not bowing properly to the guard. They were compelled to kneel ramrod-straight for long hours, their weight on knees and toes. To these men – already weak, sick and thirsty – such inhuman treatment was unbearable. When a man could no longer stand the torture and fell over, he was shot.

Prisoners were beaten every day, often without provocation. Arms were sometimes broken, or the body badly bruised by the vicious blows.

Camp chaplains were not immune to the sadistic treatment. One day, as Chaplain Zerphas walked across the compound yard on his way to the hospital ward, a guard rushed out of a sentry house and began beating him. The chaplain fell to the ground, but the guard continued kicking him in the groin, and even tried to stomp his head, missing by only inches. Then he stopped and walked back to the sentry hut.

The commandant often inflicted mass punishment for an offense committed by one person. He withheld the meager food ration or ordered all the prisoners to stand at strict attention for hours in the hot sun. On more than one occasion, when a member of a ten-man squad escaped, the other nine were shot as a reprisal. The commandant said it was done as an example for all the troops.

Once nine men were waiting in the guardhouse for execution, when the tenth man's body was discovered underneath one of the buildings where he had crawled to die. He was clutching the uneaten portion of a dead rat.

Another time two medical corps men on night duty in the hospital ward were condemned to die because during the night a psychopathic patient had escaped from their ward. Colonel Gregg called on the Japanese commandant daily for a week on behalf of the condemned men. Each time he argued their innocence, but apparently to no avail. Finally, only one hour before the two were to be shot the colonel accepted the blame himself and the commandant commuted the sentence to six months in solitary. However, it was only a face-saving gesture. Both men later were beaten to death.

Word of Colonel Gregg's selfless assumption of responsibility quickly spread through the camp, and he became a hero. The fact that one man would risk execution for his men greatly lifted camp morale.

There were days of murder and intense suffering, hours of horrible anticipation when anything could happen, and usually did. Most of the men felt as though their lives were in some great lost and found, with no one to make a claim on them.

During those trying times, Taylor often wondered what the reaction would be if the nations of the world could see Cabanatuan Compound.

Early one day in May 1942, Taylor accompanied Colonel Gillespie and Dr. Gregg to appeal to the commandant for food. He simply replied, "Arimasen!" (There is none!) But the camp leaders knew food was plentiful. The commandant was simply reflecting the attitude of the Japanese high command in Tokyo toward the American prisoners.

"You our enemy," the commandant added. "You always be our enemy, and will not be treated as prisoners of war, but as enemies!' Then he turned and swaggered away.

Starvation reaped a terrifying harvest throughout the Philippines – in Cabanatuan, O'Donnell and Bilibid – as thousands of American and Filipino soldiers continued to die from lack of food or from disease complicated by malnutrition. Survivors suffered ill effects from vitamin deficiencies, and the doctors believed they would continue to be affected for years to come.

Every privation imaginable existed in Cabanatuan – and even some the prisoners couldn't imagine.

One of the most disturbing, from the standpoint of morale, was the lack of toilet paper. There was no sanitary way to remove human waste so they used dirt. When a piece of paper did find its way into camp it was used at the latrine and on both sides, for no one knew when there would be any more.

Some of the bed patients would go to the latrine early in the morning but would be too weak to return. It was common to see them huddled near the latrine, shivering from chills, waiting for a detail to bring a litter and return them to their bamboo beds.

Amid the great trial of imprisonment acts of kindness by the American prisoners and the sense of dignity which surrounded them became commonplace. It was not unusual to see a trooper give his own medicine to a buddy who seemed to need it more. There were cases where men gave away their drugs to a friend who had a certain disease, only later to die themselves with the same disease.

The chaplains and doctors often discussed the cruel situation.

"There's really no explanation why the Japs treat us so rotten," Dr. North once told a group. "But in many ways I guess they treat their own troops cruelly."

Taylor wondered if the Japanese had inferior feelings due to their short stature and slight build. Most of the Americans were much larger, so maybe the Japanese were trying to prove themselves by subduing them.

"They think, the more we are mistreated and the weaker we become, the easier we'll be to handle," Dr. Gregg said.

Day after day, Cabanatuan continued to be the closest thing to hell every inflicted up the American fighting men.

Since the treatment by the guards was so erratic, the prisoners never knew what to expect from one day to the next. There were times when water was plentiful. Then, for no reason at all, it would be limited, and a man would be lucky if he received a pint each day. Without water the hospital became a morgue. Patients died like flies. The doctors, sick themselves, worked harder to save as many lives as possible. Their heroic work wrote a new chapter in the history of the medical profession. When anyone approached the hospital he could hear the screams of the men being operated on without anesthesia and with crude equipment, but under the skillful hands of committed men.

Sanitary conditions were nonexistent, even in the hospital. Men lay in their own excreta, and the doctors often brought dirt into the wards to cover it up.

Men ate anything they could find. Grasshoppers were a rare delicacy. Sometimes they were eaten raw, and at other times cooked until they sizzled. The men devoured them, and then licked their fingers.

Gloom pervaded the camp. Taylor heard no laughter, and the lewd stories straight from the girlie books, had long since disappeared. The men thought only of food and survival.

During the first few months in Cabanatuan the Japanese would not allow the burial detail to identify the bodies, so no records could be kept. Every morning the burial squad would find a row of bleached bodies waiting in the sun to be buried, their dog tags mysteriously gone.

By mid-May the life expectancy in Cabanatuan was nineteen days. But the imminence of death and the bizarre treatment by the guards never destroyed the desire of the prisoners to help their buddies.

One young boy named Joe, who came from New Mexico, had served with the 200th Coast Artillery. He had escaped from the barbed-wire enclosure and, because he resembled the Filipinos in appearance, went unharmed. He was living the life of a free man when he learned that the other nine men in his ten-man squad were to be killed. He returned to the camp and surrendered.

The guards decided to make an example of him. They beat him repeatedly in front of the other prisoners, and then paraded him through the camp with a sign hanging from his neck which read "I Tried to Escape." A few days later he was beheaded. The Japanese believed any man who was beheaded would never be reunited with his soul, and thus could never enter heaven. Therefore, they saved decapitation for those they hated most or anyone who embarrassed them or caused them to "lose face."

Rumors in Cabanatuan kept the morale fluctuating. The first rumor, straight from Hole Number One, said that on July Fourth an American bombing raid would take place, followed by land rescue.

July Fourth finally arrived, and at sunset some prisoners still searched the skies for sight of American bombers. They never came, and a new wave of despondency swept throughout the camp.

With the approach of the rainy season the troops experienced a new kind of misery. Lightning split the darkness at night, wind tore at the barracks by day. Taylor soon learned that the tropical rains were quite different from the gentle showers back in East Texas. He found them unmerciful and terrifying, pouring down with maddening persistence.

At night, as he lay in his bunk staring at the grass roof, he tried to kill time by letting his thoughts wander back home. He hadn't heard from his wife Ione or his family since the war began. Had they given up hope?

He rose up in bed and watched the other men in the barracks resting in silence and listening to the rhythmic beating of the rain. He lay back trying to remember what it would be like to taste a chocolate bar or apple pie or see a movie with Ione, and finally falling into a deep sleep.

The incurables – especially those in the Pearly Gates Ward – continued to prey on Taylor's mind. He heard the doctors say it was only a matter of time before 90 percent of the sick and wounded in the hospital, nearly 2000 men, died unless they received drugs. That would take a miracle.

The next day after lunch, he paused at the portico and looked across the dusty compound. The camp gates swung open and the work-detail wagon, pulled by two water buffaloes, trudged slowly back into the compound. As the detail passed, a young corporal called to Taylor, "Hi, Captain. Nice day, ain't it?"

Taylor nodded, stepped out from under the portico and walked behind the corporal.

"I'm Chaplain Preston Taylor."

"My friends call me Winky," the corporal relied.

"Winky, where does your detail work?" Taylor asked innocently as though passing the time of day.

"In the railroad yard in Cabanatuan."

"What do you do most of the day?"

"Oh, haul supplies from the railroad station, clean up debris, even unstop a sewer now and then."

"Do you have much contact with the Filipinos?"

"Not much."

"Never?"

"Well, sometimes," the corporal said.

"When?"

"Most of the time we unload boxcars, but every now and then the Fils do it. Why? What's up?"

"You're the man."

"For what?"

"Medicine!" Taylor looked around cautiously. Three guards were talking excitedly, waving their hands and only occasionally glancing at the atap palm enclosures.

"Medicine? We can't get medicine."

"The guerrillas – they can get it for you," Taylor said. "Ask the Filipinos to make contact with Clara Phillips. Spread the word around that Americans are dying like flies and there's going to be wholesale death unless the people outside get us some medicine."

New arrivals at Cabanatuan had brought word of Clara Phillips' guerrilla activity. Taylor had heard of her directly from a dying signal-corps sergeant who had been assigned to her guerrilla band.

When Bataan fell, Clara Phillips found a passport issued to a Spanish woman who had been killed in the bombings. After forging the passport picture, she moved into the Spanish hacienda in San Fernando Pampanga. Rumor was that she had been able to stay on good terms with the Japanese by supplying food from her plantation. By night, however, she scrounged medicines for guerrillas and prisoners. Her code name was "High Pockets." Already she had become a legend in Pampanga, Tarlac, and Nueva Ecija provinces.

"Gee, I don't know, Chaplain. If we get caught, we'll be shot."

"If we don't get the drugs, there'll be no hope for the bed patients or for you or me if we get sick. We'd just as well be shot," Taylor argued.

"Chaplain, they may not have any drugs," the corporal objected.

"Claire Phillips will get them for you. We've got to have medicines, and quick," Taylor replied.

"I guess we can try," Winky conceded, "but I'm making no promises."

"That's all I can ask," Taylor said. One of the guards strolled slowly toward the atap palm structures, so Taylor decided it was time to return to the hospital wards.

About midafternoon the next day he stepped outside for a breath of fresh air. He could clearly see the entire drill field and exercise yard. Several hundred prisoners, mostly older men, milled about listlessly. Most of the younger men had already died. They had been the first to lose heart and ultimately the will to live.

Weak with dysentery, many of the men were unable to walk, yet not sick enough to be committed to the hospital. Most of them just lay quietly in their handmade bunks waiting for any food the Japanese might give them.

From a quick examination of the shadows falling across the yard from the guard towers on the west side of the compound, Taylor reckoned it was nearly time for the work detail to return, but an eternity passed before he finally saw the huge wooden gate open and the ugly heads of the two water buffaloes appear as the corporal urged them forward with a short stick.

"As the carts passed the hospital, Taylor joined the procession and asked, "Well, any luck?"

"No. The Fils don't think it possible to contact the guerrillas. There's plenty of medicine to be bought, but even if we contact the guerrillas, they have to have money."

"Money," Taylor muttered. "The whole world is coming to an end and we need money."

"If you can find any of the green stuff, I'll talk to them again. But I can't promise even then that they'll be able to help us."

Taylor returned to the hospital where he sought out Colonel Oliver, Morris day, Bill Dawson and Zerphas. They made arrangements to meet in Oliver's barracks immediately after supper, if there was any. Each man entered the barracks nonchalantly from different entrances, and by eight they were all assembled.

"Now, Preston, what've you got?" Oliver asked.

"Maybe nothing, sir, but today I talked to a corporal who leads one of the work details in and out of the railroad yards at Cabanatuan, and I asked him to contact the guerrillas and Clara Phillips to see if they could get drugs into the camp. But he thinks it will take money. They say the medicines can be bought, but they have to have money." Taylor's eyes fixed on the older chaplain's face but it was Morris Day who responded.

"There must be some money in the camp. Some have it buried, others have it sewn into the linings of their clothes." Oliver agreed to pass the word among the officers and men that any money they had in Cabanatuan was needed to buy medicine for the sick.

The next day Oliver contacted Colonel Gillsepie, the ranking American officer in the camp, and he enthusiastically endorsed the proposal. Immediately the plan, code-named "Operation Life," went into action, and during the first day more than 3000 pesos were turned in to Colonel Gillespie, who buried it in a large glass jug just behind his barracks. In the days ahead the amount doubled, and they also received thirteen college and high-school rings, sixty pieces of silverware, and two pairs of glasses.

Colonel Gillespie took the knives to Colonel Schwartz for use in the hospital. The forks and spoons and two pairs of glasses were buried beside the jar of money until the time when it would be given to the work detail.

Word came down through channels to Oliver that the amount of money had increased to about 8000 pesos, and Colonel Gillespie thought that would be enough, along with the rings, silverware and glasses, to start buying the drugs.

The next afternoon Taylor waited for the work detail to return and again joined Winky as he prodded the water buffaloes across the compound yard.

"We've got money – 8000 pesos, a bunch of rings and even some silverware and glasses. It ought to buy a lot of medicine. But you've got to get word to Clara Phillips. Hundreds of lives depend on it right now."

"I'll do the best I can," Winky assured Taylor, and it was arranged that the money would be brought to the corral sometime during the night and buried just at the back of the center structure.

9.

HOPE

Although the guards noticed nothing unusual, a thousand pairs of eyes hawked the work detail when it entered the gates the next afternoon. And as it passed by the hospital, Taylor joined them and headed toward the atap palm enclosures.

Winky nodded his head twice, signaling the success of the mission.

"We got it," he said.

"Where is it?" Taylor asked.

"Between the rice bags," the corporal answered. "When it's unloaded on the rice-room floor, we'll separate it and bury it in two different places. There's lots of it and plenty more where this came from if we can get the money."

Quickly he briefed Taylor on the exact locations of the sites chosen for storing the drugs. The chaplain memorized the places and walked back to the hospital with a lighter heart. He was impressed with the wisdom of the young corporal for deciding to bury the drugs in different locations, for if the Japanese should find one there would still be the other.

When word reached Colonel Gillespie that the drugs had entered the compound, he immediately summoned Taylor.

"You pulled it off, Chaplain," the colonel said, gripping Taylor's hand firmly.

"The corporal and the work detail deserve the credit, sir. I just encouraged them," Taylor replied.

"Anyway, for the first time in months, there has been a breakthrough and lives will be saved," the colonel added. "Now, where do we find the pickup points?"

Taking a crusty strip of paper sack, Taylor with a piece of charred wood, began drawing a crude map. Carefully he pin-pointed the areas where the drugs were to be buried.

"The first pickup point is behind the atap palm enclosures, in the exact place where the money was buried," Taylor explained.

"The second point is just behind Pearly Gates, since the guards don't go near there anyway."

"Is that all?" the colonel asked impatiently.

"No, the third is a tough one, sir. The sulfas, quinine and some other drugs are hard to get. They will be passed on to the guerrillas, and we'll have to send someone out to the river at night to pick them up," Taylor explained.

"The river! We've never broken anyone loose. It's impossible," Colonel Gillespie replied skeptically.

"Winky thinks he can handle it. He's small, can get wire snips, and knows the river road beyond the cemetery like the back of his hand." Taylor answered.

"No, it's too risky."

"Sir, it's all been risky. Bringing the medicine into the camp is forbidden under penalty of death. We've got to give the corporal a go at it."

The colonel paced back and forth across the room, shaking his head slowly as if to say the attempt was too dangerous. Then he turned abruptly.

"Okay, we'll try it."

Taylor breathed a sigh of relief, took leave of the colonel and went to Barracks Number Seven, where

Winky was quartered, to give him the colonel's decision.

"You really think you can handle it?" Taylor asked.

"Yeah, the Nips think this place is impenetrable, but it ain't.

One of my buddies slipped out twice a couple of months ago and wouldn't have returned but he heard the Japs were going to shoot the rest of us. It can be done, Chaplain. Don't worry." The little corporal's confidence reassured Taylor.

"Where will you drop it?"

"I won't. I'll take it up the road to Cabanatuan near a little stream where we stop the water buffalo to drink. I'll bury it there and pick it up the next day on the way back in."

"For a guy who was so afraid of this, you really came around," Taylor said with a slight smile.

"Just needed a little prod, sir, a little prod, that's all I needed."

"When do you plan to go through the wire?"

"The Fils say the guerrillas will be at the river Saturday night just after midnight. I'll be back before daybreak."

"Okay, Corporal, and God go with you."

"He always has, sir, always has."

After lights out on Saturday night, Winky tried to rest, but sleep didn't come easily. Now that the zero hour had arrived, it was quite unlike what he had expected. Heroics and courage, he discovered, weren't the most essential equipment for this assignment. Just steel nerves.

Going over the fence was out he reminded himself on Friday as he stood in the prison yard, but he could go under like the boy from A Company.

Just at midnight he slipped out of Barracks Seven and crouched at the west end, timing the raking light from the guard tower. He waited three seconds and then dashed for the barbed-wire fence. The 12-foot structure was no stranger. He knew it like the rattle of his dog tags. He had even dreamed about the sixteen strands and the four extra strands at the top facing inward at a 45-degree angle.

A barb pricked his back as he tried to squeeze under the first strand and his hand felt the moist blood running down his side as he searched for the pliers - the precious, rusted pliers, smuggled into camp by his work detail.

High-pitched, staccato voices pierced the humid darkness around the well-lit split-bamboo nipa hut which housed the night command. Then all was quiet again.

"No sake tonight, too quiet. Must be playing Nip chess," Winky thought. They called it shogi, and the camp scuttlebutt had it that the commandant was Number One.

The guard completed his circle around the barracks and stopped between numbers Six and Seven. Removing his jungle cap, he wiped the sweat from his face, then with distinct, heavy plods, mechanically continued his rounds.

As though timed to the guard's disappearance, the light reappeared, passing within three feet of the lifeless profile half-buried in the dust, half-entangled in the wire. The beam retraced its path, carefully examining each dancing little shadow, and then moved out of sight.

The pliers bit into the taut wire. It snapped, whistling through the darkness and curling into a perfect spiral at the foot of the tower.

Sinking deep into the dust, Winky's ghostlike form waited for the ubiquitous sentry to yell "tomare," the encompassing order intended to halt all movement. But when no guard appeared, he wormed his way through the thick black dust and crawled across the narrow stone road which had been built by the prisoners with rocks carted from the river just below the cemetery to the north.

He crawled in and out of a maze of jagged bamboo stumps, silent sentinels of the bamboo thicket that once shaded the northern approach to the camp. He kissed the pliers, carefully placed them in an open bamboo stump, and then disappeared into the cogon grass that surrounded Cabanatuan Prison Compound.

The shoulder-length grass scratched his arms and bare legs as he searched frantically for the road he knew led down to the river. For eight months he had watched the patient, plodding carabao walk up and down the road, pulling the wooden-wheeled carts back and forth to the river, hauling rock and bamboo poles to be used in the camp. He reached a small clearing, stumbled and fell across a mound of fresh dirt. Looking up, he saw the silhouette of a cross dimly outlined in the moonlight. It cast a gray shadow across his face.

Scrambling to his feet, he walked confidently down the long rows of crosses, assured that even the most adventurous guard would not wander near the burial grounds at night. At the far end of the cemetery he stepped onto the road and ran toward the river several hundred yards away. The rocks clawed at his bare feet. His lungs ached and sharp pains pierced his side. He was already late for the contact, and the guerrillas, he had heard, were touchy about waiting.

Soon the shallow water rippling across the jagged rocks told him he was nearing the edge of the river, and he stopped under a large malabunga tree near the bank. Easing down the olive and gray trunk, he lay quietly looking up at the first branches 30 feet high. Two monkeys, hidden somewhere in the thick branches above his head, exchanged cries. A wild boar surreptitiously trotted toward the riverbank, then, smelling an unfamiliar scent, scurried to safety in the underbrush.

Suddenly something cold touched the back of Winky's neck. He froze in fear, certain that a python had slithered down the tree and was about to strike. He swatted at his neck above his left shoulder, but his hand was caught in the viselike grip of a smiling little Filipino, who was holding a bolo knife between the corporal's ear and the back of this neck.

"Hello. I Domingo."

"Where's the medicines?"

"Across the river," the little man answered, as three other guerrillas, their round faces beaming under their wide-brimmed hats, appeared from nowhere. One carried a .25-caliber Japanese army rifle. Three bandoleers of ammunition crisscrossed his small frame bending him toward the ground. The others, like Domingo, carried only bolos.

The middle of the river was only waist-deep. A cloud concealed the five figures as they waded across the river, drifting down-stream a few yards before reaching the opposite bank. When they stepped out of the water, four other men and two women met them and led them down a narrow path to a grove of mango trees.

"Hello," a voice greeted in perfect English from the

darkness. "I'm Clara Phillips."

"I'm Winky. Have you got the medicines?"

"Yes, and I hope we're not too late."

She handed Winky a tattered army pack, shook his hand, and as quickly as they had appeared, the guerrilla party disappeared into the jungle. The meeting had lasted only fifteen minutes.

Winky turned back down the jungle trail, forded the stream where he had crossed before, and walked toward the road that would lead him once again past the cemetery and to the camp.

When he reached the bamboo clearing, he again timed the spotlights and then crawled across the stone road toward the fence. The guard was out of sight, and he slipped under the fence where the wire had been cut, fearful that the opening had been discovered and that the guards were even now waiting for him. Stealthily he slipped across the yard and ran between Barracks Seven and Eight and around to the back, where he buried the drugs. Then he returned to the barracks undiscovered.

When the prisoners in Cabanatuan heard that medicines had been brought in, morale soared. The hospital patients were the first to receive the drugs and responded favorably. Some were even cured. For others it was already too late, but the death rate dropped to a dozen or more per day.

Each day the doctors waited patiently for the return of the work detail. Dramatic methods were contrived to hide the drugs from the all-seeing eyes of the Japanese sentries, and the doctors seemed to delight in their trickery. The hospital corpsmen detached to pick up the medicines each day became expert in diversion, feigning illness or whatever was necessary to carry out their assignment. They had some close calls, but the lifeline remained open.

For weeks the drugs poured into camp - sulfa, quinine, anesthetics, chloroform, and even some that were not labeled. With these, the doctors had to learn to experiment, careful not to prescribe too much initially until they found out exactly what drug they were handling. Fortunately no complications developed, but several times Dr. Schwartz breathed a sigh of relief as he saw a patient begin to respond to the medicine.

As the work detail became more daring, they conceived a plan for smuggling a shortwave radio into camp. They heard that they could purchase one in Manila for 7000 pesos, so once again the prisoners were asked to donate money. Although it took a little longer than it had to raise the money for the medicine, in a few weeks the pesos came in to Colonel Gillespie's office.

The work detail brought the radio into camp a piece at a time.

Only a few of the officers actually ever knew where it was kept, and camp rumor said it shifted from barracks to barracks, back to the hospital, to a hole in the ceiling, in a carefully planned attempt to keep its whereabouts secret.

Immediately the radio operator made contact with a band of guerrillas working in and around the Sierra Madre Mountains to the east. Jubilation spread through the camp when the men first heard that General MacArthur had begun his trip back to the Philippines and had already carried out hit-and-run raids on the Marshall, Gilbert and Marcus islands. Men's faces lit up over the news that early in that year of 1942 a fleet of sixteen B-25 army bombers led by Colonel James H. Doolittle took off from the carrier Hornet and bombed Tokyo 650 miles away.

The guerrilla radio reported that fifteen of the planes had run out of fuel and could not reach bases in China, but one did land safely in Siberia. The Chinese underground helped Doolittle and sixty-three of his fliers escape. Eight were executed by the Japanese.

It became commonplace for various officers to request certain items needed in the camp. The Cabanatuan radioman would ask the guerrillas to see if they could find a requested item, and if so, they were asked to pass it on to Clara Phillips.

Taylor let it be known that he wished he had a Greek New Testament. A simple request, but it proved disastrous. Shortly after the request was sent through, Clara Phillips was apprehended and a large cache of medicine and other supplies were confiscated. The Japanese Inspector General from Manila found a request from the guerrillas in the mountains for a Greek New Testament for Chaplain Taylor. Putting two and two together, the inspector guessed that Taylor and eleven other men whose names he found on various pieces of correspondence had been in contact with the guerrillas.

The twelve men were arrested.

A guard shoved Taylor into the commandant's office and ordered him to stand at attention in front of the round table that served as Captain Suzuki's desk.

At first no one spoke. Suzuki, taller than most Japanese, stared at the chaplain through horn-rimmed glasses. The muscles in his jaw flexed. He lifted this saber from its scabbard and placed it on the table in front of him. Taylor knew he must be a dreadful sight standing there in front of the Japanese. His red hair hadn't been cut in weeks; his six-foot frame was mostly skin. He wore only a pair of army shorts, the only possession not confiscated by the guards.

"Tanaka yonde kure!" Suzuki ordered, sending for the camp interpreter.

Tanaka, the little interpreter, ran in, his saber clanking against his belt buckle. He saluted his superior and stood looking at the prisoner.

Taylor watched him out of the corner of his eye. The prisoners had seen him operate - always emotional, beating the information out of prisoners when they failed to tell him what he wanted to know.

"Ha so, Kyapitan Tayror. You are sorprished. You honorably discovered by honorable Nipponjin inspector," Tanaka bellowed.

Taylor still had no idea of why he had been arrested.

"What is your name?" Captain Suzuki began the questioning through the interpreter.

"Captain Robert Preston Taylor, Thirty-first Infantry, serial number 0384411," Taylor answered, knowing that was all the Geneva Convention required.

"When did you contact the guerrillas?"

"I made no contact with the guerrillas."

"Did you leave the camp?"

"No."

Taylor knew it was capital offense to leave the prison compound and wondered if they had discovered Winky.

"Iie, denakatta," the interpreter informed the captain, who seemed satisfied with the answer. Besides, he was confident no one could slip out of his compound, and if they had they would have been foolish to return. Nevertheless, he continued the questioning.

"You, Tayror, army bokushi, you no tell lie," Tanaka ordered. Taylor knew that the word bokushi meant preacher. Since the little Jap interpreter had never been able to pronounce the r-sounds in the word "preacher," he always used the Japanese word in derision.

Immediately he repeated, "Bokushi, tell where you contact guerrillas?"

"I repeat, I did not contact them."

Captain Suzuki mumbled something under his breath.

"Kyapitan Suzuki he say, in ten minutes you no tell how you contact guerrillas, you army bokushi die," Tanaka announced.

The ten minutes passed. Captain Suzuki rose, gripped his sword, and held the point under Taylor's chin. The guard's slant eyes rounded as they waited expectantly for the punishment to be meted out on the spot. He raised the saber, then hit Taylor across the face with the handle, knocking him to the floor. The guards immediately hustled him to his feet.

"You go soritari now. The you die."

The guards dragged him out of the hut and headed toward solitary - the heat boxes, the Japanese invention for sweating the "truth" or "confession" out of the prisoners. It was placed about 500 feet from the main camp so the guards wouldn't be bothered when the prisoners lost their minds and began to scream and claw the bamboo walls.

Taylor knew that few men ever returned from solitary, and most of those who did were only vegetables - senseless, aimless, destroyed. There were a few still in the hospital, but they weren't expected to live.

The guards examined several cells and stopped in front of the fourth. From inside, a glass-eyed young prisoner crouched like a dog on all fours and gazed out the front bamboo bars as the guards shoved Taylor into the cell. They locked the door and, still talking about the baka na, fool American, returned to their posts.

The prisoner in the cell was less than twenty, but after eight months' imprisonment he looked middle-aged. He stared blankly at Taylor and managed a faint smile: " So you got the hellhole too? What did they do, catch you saying your prayers?" His voice was edgy and he had a hacking cough.

Taylor, returning the smile, replied, " It could be worse."

For a few moments the boy pondered the chaplain's words, then asked, "After you go to hell, where's the next stop?"

Taylor quickly changed the subject by asking, "What's your name, soldier?"

"Ben, but my friends call me Benny."

"Can I call you Benny?"

"Sure. What do I call you?"

"Taylor, Preston Taylor."

10.

THE HEAT BOX

The enclosure was four feet high, five feet long, and contained one blanket for each inmate. Perhaps if it had been better constructed, it would have resembled a casket. But Taylor knew no one would be so fiendish as to bury the dead in a casket that small. He tried to lie down, but he had to curl his legs in order to fit. The rancid odors caused him to gag. Maggots crawled under the blanket, and bluebottle flies swarmed in and out the cracks in the walls. The mosquitoes began silently floating in and out searching for new blood. The dim lamp hanging in front of the cell revealed their antics - diving, circling, then retreating to dive again. They infiltrated every inch of the cell. Taylor knew that only at daylight would the little tormentors grant a reprieve.

He pulled his blanket across his face, hoping to shut out the unwanted visitors, but soon abandoned the idea. Vermin, heat and hunger pangs made him too miserable to succumb to his dull drowsiness. Finally, the first rays of morning sunlight drove away the myriads of mosquitoes, it was 5 A.M. A guard doused the coal-oil lamp in front of the heat boxes, looked in on the two prisoners and walked away.

The sun is ninety-three million miles away from most places, but not from Cabanatuan. It was right on top of them, causing the heat boxes to become sweltering. Lack of ventilation made breathing hard. The sun beamed through the split walls. Benny looked out the front bars and saw a detail, a prisoner flanked by two guards, approaching the cell, but as they came closer, Taylor recognized Chaplain Morris Day, flanked by four Japanese guards.

"Preston, I've brought your things," Day said. "Have a rough night, eh?"

"Not so bad," he answered in a muffled tone. Chaplain Day eyed the guards, who seemed to be getting a little nervous.

"Preston, Colonel Gillespie and the new exec called on Suzuki this morning. He's plenty mad and may try to make it rough on you."

"New exec?"

"Yeah, a new colonel, Harold Johnson, came in with a batch of prisoners."

"Hope he's like Gillespie."

"Preston, the Japs have asked for volunteers for a work detail down on Mindanao. They want four hundred and fifty men."

"What for?"

"I'm not sure but Bill Dawson and I have volunteered."

Taylor felt a premonition that he would never see his two friends again.

"Do you have to go, Morris?"

"No, but we talked to Colonel Oliver, and it just doesn't seem right for these men to go to Mindanao without a chaplain. We've heard there are dozens of other work groups there and no chaplains. The guard poked Day in the ribs with his rifle butt, grabbed the little bag out of his hand and shoved it through the front of the cell. Taylor picked it up and examined it contents. It contained his Bible, notebook, pencil and half-dozen other items the Japanese, apparently feeling they had no value, allowed him to keep.

"Take care of yourself, Preston, " Day called as the guards ordered him back to the main camp.

For Taylor, the first day in the heat box passed uneventfully. He tried to adjust to the heat of the small enclosure but found it almost impossible. He was awakened from his half sleep, half dream, when he heard a guard shout.

By noon his strength was already beginning to ebb. Somehow he managed to raise up in the cell. Benny glanced out the front and saw a squad of Japanese soldiers marching directly toward the heat boxes. "This is it!" he shouted. " The firing squad's coming!"

The other prisoners heard his warning. Some panicked and began tearing at the walls. Others, too sick to move, just lay there.

"Preach! They're coming for us. They're gonna take us away!" The chaplain's composure bothered Benny. "Don't you care?"

"Sure, Benny, I care. There's just nothing I can do about it. Our lives are in God's hands. We'll just have to leave the matter to Him."

"What God?" Benny snorted. "I haven't seen him around here lately!"

"Have you looked, Benny?"

The squad halted in front of their box. "All prisonarus out of the cellus." Taylor recognized the voice. It was Tanaka, the interpreter.

A guard unlocked the doors and the prisoners began crawling out. They were ordered to form a line facing the cells. The squad leader, seeing some of the prisoners who were unable to move still lying in the cells, muttered something to Tanaka, who repeated, "All prisonarus outo. Any prisonaru who doesn't obey order

will be shotto." Still they didn't move. A guard, finger-
ing the safety on his rifle, looked into the nearest cell,
but the stench and smell of death caused him to back
away.

The rifle bolts clicked shells into the breeches, and
the guards aimed. "Wait!" Taylor called to Tanaka.
"We'll bring them out."

Tanaka conferred with the corporal, who nodded his
approval. The prisoners broke rank and carefully removed the other men from the cells. One, they discovered, was already dead. Another, his body racked
by spasms, floundered in the dust. Even though his
stomach was empty, he continued to retch. Intermit-
tently, he shook from chills, burned from fever.
Diarrhea added to his agony, and with both hands he
tried to seize the headache that pounded his brain.

"Oh, God," Taylor whispered. "When will it end?
When will it ever end?"

"Ike!" the corporal yelled, and the guards began
prodding the prisoners toward the main prison yard.
As he marched away, Taylor looked at the men lying in
the dust in agony. Their eyes pleaded for help, but
nothing more could be done. Taylor never saw them
again. A man on the grave detail working out of the
Zero Ward said they were buried alive, unable even to
scream out their resistance. It had happened before.
When the officers protested, they were told the prisoners would have died anyway. The Japanese always
seemed anxious to hasten death. It meant one less
mouth to feed, one less body to smell.

Most of the prisoners had already formed long lines
leading from the main gate to the opposite end of the
yard. In the center was a crudely erected platform
equipped with a loudspeaker and flying the Rising Sun.

Guards, in mushroom helmets, stood every fifteen feet.

Captain Suzuki stepped from the commandant's office and swaggered down the center of the yard toward the platform. Tanaka joined him and together they walked up the four steps to the platform.

Suzuki began his tirade against America. The troops had heard it many times before and spent the time thinking of food and trying to imagine themselves in a shady paradise, sipping cool beer, far removed from the hellhole named Cabanatuan and its devilish little proprietors.

When his speech ended, Suzuki rested for a minute and poured a glass of water from a large crystal pitcher. Then, pointing to the main gate, he shouted another order. The guards opened the barbed-wire gate, and four prisoners, two colonels and two lieutenants, were led through, their hands bound tightly behind their backs. A rope tied around each man's stomach bound them together. A guard held the end of the rope. Each wore a sign around his neck which read, "I TRIED TO ESCAPE." Their bruised and bleeding faces bore silent witness to a night of punishment. Their captors, still carrying the clubs, continued to beat them across their backs as they paraded in front of the other prisoners. Apparently, one group of ten officers had tried to go through the wire. Only four returned. No mention was made of the other six.

Captain Suzuki spoke again through Tanaka. "These men no escapu. They become exampru. No one escapu from Cabanatuan."

When the four men reached the rear of the camp they were stopped and each given a shovel and ordered to dig. The sun beat down on the nondescript ranks of men trying to stand at attention. A private near Taylor fainted and was carried to the hospital.

When the depth of the graves satisfied the guards, they took the shovels from the men and ordered them to stand in front of the holes. Ten riflemen appeared from the command hut, marched to within a few paces of the prisoners and halted, standing at strict attention. Each of the condemned men was given something to drink, but they choked violently and were unable to swallow. Cigarettes were placed between their bleeding lips.

At the order from the officer the squad readied their weapons. He removed his saber from it scabbard and raised it into the air. The doomed men spit out cigarettes and held their chins high. A sinister silence crept over Cabanatuan. Only the drone of the swarming flies could be heard. The saber fell and the crack of the rifles broke the silence. Three of the men fell backward into their graves. A fourth, a big black-haired lieutenant, was purposely spared. He was hit only in the leg and knocked to the ground. Apparently he was receiving special treatment for showing belligerence to a guard. As he tried to stand, a second volley ended his torment. The officer then went to the open graves and shot each of the men between the eyes. The prisoners were dismissed. The object lesson had successfully created awesome fear in the hearts of all who witnessed the execution.

Taylor and his companions were marched back to solitary, but Taylor could not forget the faces of the dying men. He wondered about their last thoughts - home, wife, children, or just a desire to live. Maybe some even thought of God.

Dusk settled over the prison camp and mosquitoes returned.

Benny hadn't spoken since the execution. He only stared at the wall. His head jerked sharply at the sound of the guard who lit the coal-oil lamp and then walked away. Taylor pondered the day's events. He had seen hundreds of deaths, but each had its own personality, its own treachery. Then into the darkness of that supreme moment a light seemed always to shine. He had seen it in their faces. Some power had led them through the dark shadow and given them a victory that nothing - not even death -could take away.

War with the mosquitoes entered its second night. Taylor knowing that any attempt at sleep was futile, placed his blanket over Benny, then leaned against the wall dropping into a half sleep. Visions of food leaped from his subconscious, and at times he reached out to take some delectable item off an imaginary table. But the movement of his arm caused him to jerk back into consciousness and return again to his confinement. He tried to recapture the dream, but it was gone.

He decided to quote verses from the Psalms. "The Lord is my shepherd," he began. It surprised him how much energy was necessary even to quote a verse. "I shall not want," he continued. "He maketh me to lie down in green pastures." Taylor shifted his weight, trying to fit more comfortably into the bamboo structure. "He leadeth me beside the still waters." It reminded him that he hadn't had a drink in two days.

Benny pushed the blanket from his face, swatted a mosquito, and listened intently.

"He leadeth me in the paths of righteousness for his name's sake." Taylor paused and then, seeming to gain new strength, added, "Yea though I walk through the valley of the shadow of death, I will fear no evil, for thou art with me." He continued in silence for a moment, but noticing the disappointment on Benny's face, said audibly, "Surely goodness and mercy shall follow me all the days of my life and I shall dwell in the house of the Lord forever."

The cell was silent. Even the mosquitoes weren't so pesky as before. "My Mom taught me that when I was a boy, " Benny said. " I'd sure like to believe it. If only it were real."

"It's real, Benny, it's real." He watched the boy as he fell into a deep, restful sleep, apparently the first he had experienced in days.

Morning dawned and the prisoners hoped to be fed. For two days the guards had withheld water and even the small daily portion of rice. Pangs of hunger had left them days before, but the constant thirst sent some to the edge of delirium.

About midday, a sergeant from the camp mess hall brought a bucket of rice with some vegetables and carefully measured out two ounces to each prisoner. It was poor grade, scrapings from the rice-house floor.

Still, it was food and greatly lifted their morale. Benny became quite talkative. "Preach, the Bible reading last night kinda touched me down here," he said.

Taylor smiled. Reaching for his sack of personal effects, he removed a worn Bible and motioned to Benny. "You can read it anytime you wish."

The boy, nodding his thanks, said "Tell me something, Preach. I got drafted, but you volunteered for this. Why?"

Taylor searched for the right answer. Why had he come? Fort Worth was a lot safer and Ione was there. But he had been called. There was no question about that. "God led me here Benny, to help these men. He knew about this great tragedy ahead of time and wanted me here to try to give spiritual help. That's why."

He knew also the War Department wanted to provide a place for the Church and the Christian religion among the men in uniform. But it went deeper with him. He had been called. God had sent him to the Philippines for a purpose. The details hadn't all been revealed. But he was called, of that he was sure. That was his commission, his ordination, and he had no regrets.

Besides fighting the stifling heat, Taylor found he had to adjust to the monotony of the long days. The four-by-five cell cramped his body. His arms and legs were turning numb. To help alleviate this numbness, he decided on an exercise program. Sitting up, he slowly began exercising his arms. Crisscrossing them, he scissored through a routine, left over right ten times, then reversed the pattern. When he had no more energy, he massaged his legs, kneading the tough, leathery flesh, browned from constant exposure to sun and dirt.

Days turned into weeks, one uncertainty to another. During August and September the specter of death continually hovered over the heat boxes, but the guards paid little attention. Occasionally a new guard would saunter up to a cell, spit on one of the captives, then quickly retreat. The other American prisoners were of course forbidden to go near the isolated men, under penalty of death.

Since no latrines were accessible, some piled the waste in front of their cells doors, hoping to rake it out with their bare foot should the door open. Others, too weak to care, lay in their own refuse. Each day hastened the deterioration of their helpless souls.

One by one, those suffering from advanced malaria or dengue fever became too weak to eat the half-rotten sweet potatoes or drink their portion of water. When their companions yelled "Shinda! Shinda!" the guards summoned the burial squad and the body was hurried away to Zero Ward to await burial the next day.

There, reasoned Taylor, he would suffer the final indignity. Already he had been judged without trail. He was hungry without food, sick with no medicine. Now he would be buried, but no benediction would be said over his corpse.

And still the sun poured down through the open shafts of the crude enclosures. A sailor in the box next to Taylor went into delirium and began reciting the pledge of allegiance. He reached the second line and dropped into a coma; then, regaining consciousness, he began beating his head against the wall. His companion tried to comfort him, but his mind had crossed the line. He growled like a dog and gnashed his teeth at this cellmate. A series of convulsions ended in his death.

Taylor listened for further sounds of life but could hear only the frightened whimper of the cellmate, a boy of twenty-one, as he prayed for his own death. The chaplain clasped the wooden bars on the cell door and squeezed until his knuckles turned white. Whispers of doubt crept through his own mind, driving him closer to the brink of insanity. His endurance was almost gone. The end was in sight. Then he lost consciousness, and the next thing he knew, Benny was shaking him violently. "Wake up, Preach! Preach! Don't talk like that! We need you. Oh my God, we need you!"

Taylor tried to recall the past few minutes, realized that his mind had been playing tricks, and knew that he had to keep that mind busy if it were not to go completely. His Bible - that was best. Suddenly, his fears were gone, and for the first time in many weeks he felt a calm passing through his entire being like a cool breeze. He prayed to God for forgiveness of his fear. If God had a purpose for him, surely he would survive. But dying would be so much easier.

After the seventh week, Taylor noticed a slight change in the attitude of the guards. The portions of rice seemed to be getting larger, and the POWs were taken out for exercise each day. Most of the men in the heat boxes were too weak to walk, so volunteers came daily to help them from the cages and carry them to the exercise yard. There Taylor would collect a small group of men about him and read to them from the Bible, even though sometimes he had to hold onto a bamboo stick to keep from falling.

"If you could turn me inside out and look at my heart, you would see a man who still believes in the power of God," Taylor told them one day. "We have been subjected to the most depraved tortures and seen our captors violate every civilized code of the free world. The contorted forms of our dead comrades lie in shallow graves - graves that emit an odor that outrages the air. They force us to carry our buddies in and out of Zero Ward on bamboo biers. They permit us only meager water when they have plenty."

As he spoke, several other men gathered around him.

"Food, meager in quantity, inferior in grade, rice scraps cooked with water lilies - why, it would poison the pigs back in East Texas. Ten men tried to escape but were caught by their well fed pursuers, marched back to camp, forced to dig their own graves, then shot and kicked into the very graves."

His voice choked as he continued: "Open latrines create serious sanitation problems. We have no kitchen utensils, only the large iron pots for cooking rice or the husks of rice we get. Our clothes are so dirty the Japs won't touch them, and then we're subjected to the verbal abuse of a fiendish commandant who speaks to us through his roly-poly interpreter."

Several of the men chuckled as Taylor mentioned Tanaka.

"If we go within twenty paces of the fence we're shot. Some of our men have been taken to headquarters and have never come back. Then, flies and mosquitoes seek to annihilate us all."

He scanned the faces of the listening men.

"But we won't give up! Any way you cut this place it's the same old dung heap, only the flies have changed. But we'll live and we'll make this world a place where this can't happen again. The blood of our buddies in Cabantuan will not be spilt in vain. This will not become a graveyard of the nameless dead. God is going to help us survive!"

Several Japanese guards listened intently as the weakened man continued to address the growing crowd.

"Ask me about my condition. I'm dirty, nasty, and all I have on is my underwear. Can you smell the stench of my rotting teeth? Listen to me, listen without pity. I'm not going to die!"

He a shouted the last words as loudly as he was able, and a cheer went up from the listeners that brought other guards rushing from the nipa huts near the front gate.

"I'm going to live and you are too, because God is

going to give us the strength. Now bow your heads in prayer," he concluded as a half-dozen guards closed in to take him back to the heat box.

The several hundred men who had heard Taylor knew something mystical had taken place. Their allegiance, they discovered, was to God. They would never pay their dues to the little yellow company of criminals.

As on trooper later related the experience, "We still smell the urine, the outdoor privy, the accidents on the blankets, the rotting garbage we would bury if we had shovels, but we have hope. Thank God we have hope!"

Even the heat boxes somehow felt different. The cells were the same cramped hellholes, but the commandant began allowing the prisoners to receive books for reading. Ironically, one of the books that somehow made its way into Cabanatuan was Dostoevsky's The House of the Dead. Taylor marveled at the insight of a man of an earlier generation who said: "The degree to which a society is civilized can be judged by entering its prisons."

One of his favorites was A Book of Poems. From its pages he read " The Concord Hymn," and he particularly liked the verse that said:

Spirit, that made those heroes dare
To die, and leave their children free,
Bid Time and Nature gently spare
The shaft we raise to them and thee.
That Memory may their dead redeem
When, like our sires, our sons are gone.

The Bible also took on new meaning as each day passed. During the first eight weeks in the heat box, Taylor had read it through five times, and its authoritative message helped him to plumb the paradox of his cruel surroundings. Hidden in the folded cloak of its most difficult passages, he found encouragement for hope. Suddenly he discovered that the very dust in which he lay was sacred if his own heart was right and pure before God. Something inside him said that Cabanatuan would one day be an empty stage, the actors gone, and with the resurgence of spiritual hope, his body also began to gain strength.

At the end of the ninth week the guard approached the cells and ordered the prisoners to form in front. Since most of the weaker ones had already died, all but a few were able to follow the order. A Japanese corporal then led the men across the exercise field to a row of freshly cut bamboo huts, placing five in each one.

The situation continued to improve. Even the guards seemed friendlier, perhaps because after nearly a year, they too had grown weary of all the suffering and hate. But although the prisoners were grateful for the transfer to the larger cells, most of them still thought they would spend their last days in solitary, for no one had given them any indication of how long they were to be punished.

From the larger cells the men in the heat boxes were allowed to go to the water barrel and the latrine. Then suddenly, without warning, the privileges and the food ration were cut and for days the men were not allowed out of the cells. They received no food at all, only a meager ration of water, and again their condition deteriorated to the danger point. Then, on the fourth day, the guards brought some nigiri, little rice balls. The men ate the life-saving provisions as they would a great delicacy and then, again for no apparent reason, the food supply was cut.

The guards repeated the same pattern for several weeks, as though carrying out some scheme to rid themselves of all the prisoners in the heat boxes, half of them already at the point of death. Apparently, Captain Tanaka was outraged by the revived spirits throughout the camp.

When he lost the capacity to digest the small rice supply and vomited everything he tried to eat, Taylor wondered if the end had come. Dysentery taxed the strength that remained until, at last, he went into a coma.

That evening, Colonel North visited the solitary stockade. As he approached Taylor's cell, he looked inside and gasped. Frantically, he clawed at the gate, trying to tear it off so he could get inside, but a guard cracked him across his left shoulder with the butt of his rifle. Although he was stunned by the blow, North managed to get back to the hospital, where he found Colonel Schwartz. When North told him that Taylor was dead, Schwartz grabbed his medical kit and a container of water and ran to the heat boxes. Surprisingly, the guard allowed him to pass.

Schwartz opened the cell door and stepped inside. Leaning over the lifeless form, he place his ear to Taylor's chest. The heartbeat was faint, but it was there. As he started to go for help, he ran into Captain Suzuki, flanked on either side by his interpreter and his first sergeant.

"Kyapitan Suzuki say no touchu prisonaru," said the interpreter. North drew himself up, pointed his finger directly into the face of the commandant, and said, "This man is at the point of death. If he is left here, he will contaminate the other prisoners and the guards."

Captain Suzuki's eyes widened as he listened to

Tanaka, and said something in Japanese.

"Kyapitan Suzuki say you take prisonaru to hospritar to die," translated Tanaka.

11.

THE MIRACLE

Hundreds of men milled around outside the hospital ward, waiting for word about Taylor. Most of them had been in the hospital at one time or another and knew how faithfully the chaplains were trying to help the sick. Now it was their turn to reciprocate, and even when the bugle sounded lights out at nine o'clock, they refused to return to their barracks but instead defiantly sat down. Other prisoners began pouring out of the barracks to join in the vigil, and even when the tower guards clicked the bolts on their .30-caliber machine guns, the men refused to move. The guards called Captain Suzuki, who again ordered the men back to the barracks. Still they refused.

The captain shouted "Oi, dame, yo! Nanni mo shinai!" at the guards, and those who had picked up a little knowledge of Japanese knew he had ordered the guards to keep their hands off the prisoners. When the word was passed around, a great shout went up.

The event marked the first time in more than a year that the prisoners had successfully defied the Japanese. Yet, when at last they quietly returned to their barracks, all the men were aware that the reprisal might still come the next day. To their mystification, however, nothing happened.

Dr. Gregg and Dr. North worked over Taylor all through the night keeping cold cloths on his forehead and praying that he would recover. In the meantime, Chaplain Oliver sent word around the camp that Taylor, who so many times had prayed for other men, now himself needed their prayers. The men immediately responded, and a prayer vigil began which was to last for two weeks. Different barracks formed chains of prayer, with certain groups taking a given hour, then another group picking it up and continuing. On and on it went, twenty-four hours a day, and there were always ample volunteers for the night hours, when ordinarily they would have been asleep.

The doctors continued to observe Taylor carefully until one night, just at midnight, they noticed a deeper breathing, and he moved slightly. By morning he was conscious, though incoherent and under the impression that he was still in the heat box. That afternoon, however, he recognized Gregg, Oliver and North, and gradually, almost miraculously, from then on he continued to improve.

Somehow the recovery of Chaplain Preston Taylor had become a symbol of hope for all the captives. More than any other person in the prison, he had encouraged others to hope. Now his recovery foreshadowed a genuine renewal of hope in the entire camp, and when the prisoners looked at him, they saw a living answer to prayer.

Weak from dysentery, for weeks Taylor was unable to walk, but his contagious spirit of optimism reached out to everyone who came near his bed. Finally, with the aid of a bamboo cane made for him by one of the prisoners, he managed to get around the compound. Everywhere he went he was greeted with, "Hi, Chaplain. We prayed for you," or, "It's gonna be okay, Chaplain. We been talking to God." At last, after two months, Taylor was allowed to leave the hospital and return to his barracks.

On his first night back, the chaplains met. As Taylor approached Colonel Oliver's barracks, he looked through the door and for a moment thought he had lost his mind again. He wasn't sure, but the man sitting on the bamboo bunk between Zerphas and Oliver looked like Father Duffey, the little Catholic chaplain from the Death March. He rubbed his eyes and looked again. Suddenly the other man looked up, recognized Taylor and bolted from the bunk. For several minutes the two chaplains were silent, unable to express their feelings. Then Father Duffey explained that after being attacked by the guard on the march, he had been picked up by Filipinos who had nursed him back to health. For more than a year he had ministered to the mountain people until he was captured again by the Japanese.

Taylor knew that if he had died and gone to heaven, he could not be any happier than he was at this reunion with his close friend. When they went into the barracks, a new spirit of confidence and purpose permeated the conversation.

Colonel Oliver had called the meeting to discuss some important decisions he felt should be made. Changes had taken place in Cabanatuan with the increased availability of drugs from the guerillas and the resulting lower death rate in the camp. Now the chaplains needed a new approach to ministering to the prisoners, an approach that would keep morale high and help the men to occupy their minds. If a way were found, the colonel knew it would increase their chances for survival.

Zerphas suggested they renew their request to conduct open religious services on the parade ground. Taylor thought organized activities would be helpful, since the prisoners' health had improved to the point where many of them could participate.

They decided to see Captain Suzuki the next day and ask permission to begin religious services. Then, after a prayer, they returned to their own barracks.

Immediately after breakfast the next day, Colonel Oliver, Taylor and Zerphas approached Captain Suzuki's office and asked to see the commandant.

"He cannot see you today," a Japanese officer said in perfect English. "He's being returned to Japan. His successor is Major Takahashi, who will be here next week. I am Captain Watanabe.

Can I help you?"

All three men stiffened and shuffled their feet looking at each other in disbelief as they listened to the officer.

Finally Oliver said, "Yes, Captain. For more than a year we have wanted to conduct religious services for our men, but permission has been refused. We would like to ask once more for permission to conduct such a service,"

"You may have the service," the captain answered unhesitatingly. "You may have your first service in the parade yard. All the guards will also attend."

Oliver, dumbfounded, wanted to hug the little officer, but he held back. This was the first act of kindness he had witnessed on the part of the Japanese conquerors since the fall of Bataan.

"I will also attend, Colonel," the captain added. "You see, I grew up in a mission orphanage in Japan and learned English from a Christian missionary lady who was the greatest person I ever knew."

With the change in Japanese personnel came a different attitude toward the prisoners. For nearly a year and a half the compound had been ruled by battle-hardened troops, victorious in the Philippine campaign.

Now occupation troops, fresh from the mainland, were arriving. Some of them were young boys in their late teens. It gave the prisoners some idea of how the war must be going. Due to pressures in other theaters of war, the seasoned troops were being transferred.

To be sure, when it rained the captives still stood in the water, scrubbing their bony bodies and washing their ragged clothes, but they knew the worst had passed.

From the time Taylor heard the good news that the chaplains would be allowed to conduct their first combined worship service, he had offered quiet prayers of thanksgiving. Now, leaning on his bamboo cane, he slowly made his way toward the center of the compound yard and overheard the chaplains speaking to Colonel Oliver.

"It's only right for you to do it," Zerphas was saying. "The men will be expecting you to lead the service."

"But one of you younger men should conduct it," the older chaplain replied.

"What do you think, Preston?" Zerphas asked.

"Well, the men look to you, Colonel Oliver, as their spiritual leader, a sort of spiritual father," Taylor said.

"They would be greatly disappointed if you don't," Zerphas added.

Noticing that Oliver was beginning to soften, Taylor said, "We'll help you, Colonel. Zerphas can lead the hymn, Father Duffey can pray, and" he paused "and I'll read the Scripture."

"Okay. We'll do it, God be praised," the older chaplain replied.

Cabanatuan's parade ground was transformed into a great outdoor cathedral as the chaplains, accompanied by Colonel Johnson and Captain Watanabe, mounted the crude platform and faced the silent throngs of waiting men.

"Men, we've received permission to conduct our first worship service," Colonel Johnson announced. "Each of you, whether Catholic, Jew or Protestant, is invited to worship in your own way, personally, to your God. I now turn the service over to Lieutenant Zerphas, who will lead the hymn."

Zerphas approached the microphone and announced the hymn, "For the Beauty of the Earth."

"Many of you may not know this hymn," he said. "I'll go through the words with you and we'll learn the melody."

The men listened intently as he sang:

For the beauty of the earth
For the glory of the skies
For the love which from our birth
Over and around us lies.
Christ our God to Thee we raise,
This our song of grateful praise.

By the time he finished the first verse, many of the prisoners had joined him and others hummed the melody. Then they sang it again.

Most of the men stood with bowed heads as Taylor approached the microphone with his tattered Bible in his hand to read the Scripture. Without introduction he began to read. Just before he finished, Father Duffey stepped forward and stood beside him, and, when the Scripture was completed, Father Duffey began to pray.

"Our Father, we thank thee for this wonderful, memorable occasion. We thank thee for your presence with us here. We pray for the sick in the wards and for those of our friends who have passed on to their reward. Be merciful to them, dear God, as you are to us. We pray for our loved ones back in the States. Stand by them and comfort them. O God, help us to be faithful to you and to all that we believe. Lead us to trust your word and your loving care. In Jesus' name, who taught us to pray, even as he prayed."

He paused for a moment, then began the Lord's prayer. The prisoners joined him, and the voices of the beleaguered men formed a chorus that Preston Taylor knew he would never forget.

Colonel Oliver thanked the Japanese commander for allowing them to conduct the service and then, turning to the prisoners, said, "Men, I've learned never to doubt in the darkness what I believed in the light. We have all felt the presence of God here today, and a new light shines in Cabanatuan."

He scanned the longing faces of the sea of men.

"Now, men, I want to talk to you for a while about forgiveness. There are two kinds, you know, when God forgives us, and when we forgive others. If we are to find true peace with God we must forgive, even as we are forgiven."

Captain Watanabe and the camp guards listened carefully as the colonel continued.

"If we fail to forgive, then hatred can become a poison in our veins that will mark us until the day of judgment and bring spiritual death an inch at a time. But if we learn to forgive, we can find true peace with God. May God help us all to learn to forgive."

Towering cumulus clouds sailed like galleons across the Philippine sky as some of the men returned to their barracks and others stayed milling around the parade grounds.

The chaplains discussed the change that was taking place among the prisoners. They realized the potential danger inherent in such a religious awakening, for they knew that over the centuries man had used religion as a cloak to cover his fears, but when the danger passed he threw the cover away.

Many of these men, too, would do the same, Taylor knew, and yet he was convinced that the risen Christ was walking up and down the corridors of Cabanatuan.

The chaplains next launched a complete program of activities, including programs of a religious nature on certain nights as well as lectures on philosophy, history, geography and other subjects on alternating nights. All meetings opened and closed with prayer.

Most of the events that led to the transformation of Cabanatuan from a morgue to a mountaintop were spontaneous and caught even the chaplains by surprise, but the one that surprised them most was the camp orchestra. Seemingly from nowhere, more than fifty different musical instruments appeared. The Japanese, thinking that many of the old band pieces were worthless, had thrown them away. They were discovered, along with a violin, when some troops were rummaging through an old garbage heap near the camp, and the prisoners ingeniously repaired them. The work detail also brought a number of instruments from town. Some were taken from the railroad cars, others from junk piles, and still others were purchased from townspeople. In a few short weeks, the orchestra was presenting concerts, and as Christmas 1943 approached, the orchestra and choir worked long hours rehearsing a cantata. One of the prisoners had a copy of the cantata, and the choir and orchestra members labored meticulously for days copying the words and music on any scrap of paper that could be found.

The whole compound was buzzing with Christmas excitement, and when Major Takahashi, the new camp commandant, finally arrived, one of his first acts was to provide a bundle of newspapers for use in the Christmas preparations. Prisoners immediately cut them into long ribbons and pasted them together with some glue supplied by a Japanese guard.

A corporal who had worked in a leather factory back in Arizona concocted a dye from discarded Japanese shoe polish, some weeds and ink from the library. Then he carefully colored the long ribbons, and when he was finished, there were enough to decorate all the barracks and hospital wards.

Old tin cans were salvaged and the rust removed; then they were placed in doorways throughout the camp. A tinsmith in camp fashioned other cans into little stars and other decorations.

He even made a tin chandelier for Colonel Johnson's office, and all the prisoners agreed it was beautiful.

Several beautiful Christmas trees also appeared in camp, brought in by a work detail hauling rock from the Sierra Madre foothills. Rice rations were hoarded for group parties planned for Christmas Day. From somewhere the cooks scrounged a little sugar and baked some delicious rice cakes for the bed patients still in the hospital.

On Christmas morning the camp echoed with "Merry Christmas!" Morale had never been higher in Cabanatuan; even the guards managed quick smiles.

When Taylor saw the guards' response to the merry-making, he thought to himself, no man is a stranger when you get up real close. Not even a Japanese. They, too, had loved ones in their homeland, families they missed.

The choir moved from place to place through the camp singing carols, and presented brief concerts in both the main camp and the huge hospital area. Nearly all the prisoners heard them and joined in the singing of "Silent Night."

Camp wide services were also held, and although they were all prisoners of war and far from home, Taylor remarked to Father Duffey that he had never seen a more genuine Christmas spirit. It was not commercialized and stripped of its meaning.

Christmas passed, but its meaning continued in the men's hearts. The number of men attending the worship services continued to swell, and toward spring it became necessary to organize the men into various service groups to help handle all those attending the meetings. Deacons, stewards and directors were elected and called on to direct business meetings pertaining to church activities. They also lectured during the evening meetings on what laymen can do in the church.

On Easter Sunday a sunrise service was announced. Even before daybreak, hundreds of men gathered on the parade ground for worship, and just as the first rays of light broke into the camp the choir began to sing: "Christ the Lord is risen today ..."

As Taylor listened to Colonel Oliver speak on "The Living Christ," he thought of Easter services in America and wondered about the other prison camps in the Philippines. In a land where hundreds of men had died and thousands of others walked the path of death, it was awe-inspiring to have fellowship with the living, triumphant Christ.

Mother's Day was also featured with a well-organized program. The men were requested to wear a flower, a white one if their mothers were deceased, a red one if they were alive.

When the bugler sounded church call, the men came in large numbers. Many of them had no shirts, shoes or caps, but each carried a red or white flower fashioned out of newspaper and dyed in honor of his mother.

On Memorial Day they held a special service at the camp cemetery. Early in the morning, several hundred men marched, under guard, from the camp to the burial ground. In honor of men of all faiths, Catholics, Jews and Protestants participated in the service.

A Jewish soldier prayed in Hebrew, Taylor read the Scripture, and Father Duffy spoke briefly.

At the close of the ceremony, Major Takahashi placed a wreath of beautiful flowers on a tomb picked at random, then politely saluted the dead. Later they learned that when the Japanese General in Manila heard of the forthcoming Memorial Day service in Cabanatuan, he had personally sent his representative to carry the wreath, and it made Taylor wonder about the strangeness of the oriental philosophy.

Filipino guerrillas continued their work on behalf of the prisoners of Cabanatuan. They organized welfare groups in and around Manila and collected money, food and medicine for the POWs. Each week they sent as much of it as possible into the camp.

Word reached Colonel Johnson over the short-wave radio that Clara Phillips had been tried and condemned to die, but after months of brutal treatment, she was tried again and her sentence changed to life imprisonment.

Taylor thought of the Filipino martyrs who had died for the faith. They had dared to sacrifice their own safety to help prisoners of war in violation of Japanese laws. But they counted the law of Christ of greater value than the laws of men, and even the most severe punishment meted out by the Japanese could not stop these good Samaritans.

The money that came into the camp was divided among the men in the hospital who needed extra food in order to survive.

The Japanese allowed Colonel Johnson to set up a commissary and even made certain foodstuffs available to him. Most of it was native produce such as fruits, sugar and poultry. By the end of 1943, these items could be purchased for the sick, for since December 1942, the Japanese had been paying a few pesos per month to the officer personnel of the camp. Enlisted men who worked were paid fifteen centavos per day, and to support those men who could not work, the officers set up a welfare fund of five thousand pesos per month. At each commissary the welfare order received priority, and the men in the worst condition were the first to receive help.

Early in 1944, the first Red Cross packages arrived in Cabanatuan but were not distributed. The grapevine reported that the Japanese had hoarded warehouses full of these packages in Manila and used them for their own troops, but no one knew for sure.

Shortly thereafter, the Red Cross delivered the first

mail from home to the prisoners. When Major Taka-hashi announced mail call over the camp loudspeaker, the troops were almost in a state of frenzy as they sur-rounded the guard hut from which the letters were to be distributed. It took two hours to parcel out the mail. Most of the letters were closely censored.

Taylor stared in unbelief when his name was called, and felt deeply for the G.I. standing beside him who re-ceived no word from home.

It was a letter from his mother, and he took it back to Barracks Eight away from the noisy crowds.

He carefully opened it and saw that certain sections had been removed by a Japanese censor. But enough re-mained to let him know his family was well and that his wife Ione had moved to San Francisco to await his re-turn.

But as he read further the letter said, "Your Father is dead, of pneumonia. We miss him greatly. His last thoughts were of you."

After a few minutes he sensed someone standing nearby and looked up to see Bill Dawson.

"You okay, Preston?"

"Yeah, Bill. Where'd you come from?"

"Our work detail returned from Mindanao today."

"And Morris?"

"He stayed there."

"Oh?"

"Plenty of work yet to be done."

"Bill, Dad is gone, died of pneumonia."

"I'm sorry, Preston. He was a good man." The bald-headed chaplain sat down on the bunk beside Taylor. "A real good man."

"I'll miss him."

"We'll all miss him. But we'll see him again. That's

our hope, our victory. We may lose a few battles here, Preston, but God's going to win the war."

"You always seem to show up just at the right time, Mussolini."

Taylor grinned.

"I'll take good care of you, old buddy."

They talked long into the night about the work detail in Mindanao, Taylor's illness and release from the heat boxes, and the renewal which was sweeping Cabanatuan.

A few days later the prisoners received the Red Cross packages. Some contained small tins of powdered milk, and immediately a request went out from the doctors in the hospital for donations of the milk for the TB patients.

The packages also contained canned meats, vegetables, soups and other food, enough for several weeks, and soon the death rate was checked even further as the prisoners gained strength to fight off disease.

Taylor noticed that the food also brought spiritual and moral good to the hearts of the men. Everywhere men spoke of the goodness of God, for they knew the minds of the Japanese and were convinced that only divine intervention in the hearts of the Japanese leaders could have moved them to allow the food to enter the prison.

Major Takahashi also bought curacaos from the Filipinos and brought them into the compound as food for the prisoners. The meat provided badly needed proteins for their diet.

Later he granted permission to start a huge farm just outside the wall, where the prisoners planted eggplant, capote, a native sweet potato, sweet corn and cucumbers.

From time to time, coconuts and bananas were brought into camp by Japanese supply trucks or POW work details, and one day some flour was received. The ingenious prisoners built ovens out of old oil barrels, and the cooks made some of the most delicious bread the prisoners had ever tasted.

Later the Japanese brought chickens into camp, five per five hundred men, and issued fifty eggs per five hundred men. The cooks made soup, and all the eggs went into it. Starvation and malnutrition were reduced greatly during the ensuing months, and the condition of the entire camp improved.

When the gnawing hunger from his runaway appetite was finally curbed, Taylor often thought of the men for whom the food was too late. He knew that as long as he lived he would remember with horror the days and months of starvation during which so many of his friends had died.

With their physical strength renewed, the men also began to take more interest in the sanitary conditions in the camp. They dug deeper latrines and scrounged enough rough lumber to build seats over the open trenches. When the rains came, the trenches still filled with water, but it was much better than before, even though they could find no way to confine the maggots to the trenches.

The work details continued to be masters at procuring food and other needs. With the relaxed controls, the guards no longer performed the shakedowns on all the prisoners coming back into the camp, so the men sewed false pockets in their clothing, tied articles around their waists, and even placed them under their armpits. One of the prisoners went through the routine inspection with twenty-six fish, weighing approximately sixteen pounds. Two of the fish were concealed in his hat.

The Japanese guards, particularly the officers, removed most of the restrictions by which the prisoners had been so severely governed. It was not uncommon to see prisoners talking freely with the guards, trying to explain English, trying to understand Japanese, both parties gesticulating fiercely.

Taylor conversed freely with Captain Watanabe. Several times the Japanese captain invited him for tea in the commandant's office. Their conversations ranged from political philosophy to religion and often touched on war and peace, Japanese psychology and even death.

"Japanese people are very stoical about death," the captain said one day. "In the Orient the death rate is so high most Orientals don't look on it as you Americans do."

"How do you think Americans look on death?

"I know how you look at it. The missionary woman in Japan took the little orphan children, babies no one else wanted, some sick and better off dead," Watanabe explained. "Out here the attrition among infants is so great and the life expectancy so short why be concerned about it?"

Taylor pondered the question seriously before replying, "Most Americans follow the Christian teachings and believe that each person is created in the image of God and therefore has a personal importance that even death cannot destroy."

"But not all Americans follow Christian teachings" Watanabe said. "Before the war I saw the American foreign service personnel in the bars and geisha houses, and the young sailors from the ships in Japanese bars."

"Oh, I didn't say all of them followed the teachings

of the Christian way. I said most of them believed it, and there is a vast difference."

"Oh?"

"When a person believes in something in his head, it greatly influences what he does and the way he reacts to given situations, including death," Taylor explained. "But when a person commits himself to that way, above every other way, it changes him and the way he acts."

Watanabe sipped his ocher and munched on a somber rice cracker, apparently confused by Taylor's explanation.

"The gods, all the gods, have been good to my country," he said.

"Oh? What gods?"

"In 1281, Kublai Khan organized an armada to defeat Japan, which had been a thorn in his side. My country faced impending doom. Then a typhoon hit and destroyed the Khan's armada. We Japanese call it the kamikaze, divine wind. It will always protect my country. It is one of our gods. The gods gave us a beautiful land, among the last unspoiled paradises left on earth, strewn like a handful of jewels on wind-tossed hills and cloud-capped mountains. And for three thousand years the outside world has not shattered our island serenity. Yes, Chaplain Taylor, the gods favor us."

"The whole universe speaks of one God, a Divine Creator. We see him in the stars and in man's conscience," Taylor replied.

"Our gods speak in the wail of the Bugrake at Meiji Shrine, in the misty vistas of the piney picture islands in the Inland Sea, in the Noh drama from ancient times and kabuki, theater of the seventeenth century. These are our gods. The sumo, gargantuan wrestlers, begin each bout by scattering salt to rout demons. These are the gods of the Japanese."

Taylor took his leave a short time later, secretly thankful his faith was in a living God rather than a divine wind.

On September 21, 1944, at 9 a.m., Taylor was visiting patients in the hospital wards when he heard cheering from the parade ground. Going outside he saw huge squadrons of American planes appear over the Sierra Madre Mountains. Within seconds, the planes roared over above Cabanatuan. Camp morale sky-rocketed. That night the radio broadcast said more than a thousand American bombers, some from one of Admiral Halsey's carriers, had taken part in a raid on Japanese airstrips in and around Manila. The report said the Japanese air force had been virtually wiped out.

The next day more planes appeared. It was a clear day, and the prisoners could easily see the planes were Navy dive bombers.

The Japanese guards just looked at them and said nothing.

They didn't even admit they were American.

For more than two years the prisoners had longed for the sight of American planes. Now that the hour had come they felt sure they would soon be liberated.

But the bombings forced the Japanese high command in Tokyo to rethink its Philippine strategy, and their new plan would greatly affect the officers and enlisted men who for two years and three months had survived in Cabanatuan.

Taylor returned to his routine duties, one of which was the redistribution of New Testaments that had belonged to men who had died. The chaplains gave them out upon request.

Others were placed at central locations in all barracks and hospital wards, so that anyone who desired would have access to the Word of God.

Hundreds of men met for Bible study each Wednesday night.

It was apparent that the teachings of the Scriptures had become an integral part of camp life in Cabanatuan, and when one man dared use several pages from a New Testament to roll his cigarettes, a group of men from his own barracks talked to him.

He never did it again. The men never told the chaplains what they had said, but whatever it was, it worked.

Some of the men still carried Bibles their parents had given them when they left the United States, and they prized them greatly.

One day a soldier approached Taylor and said, "Chaplain, I have a Bible here, and I don't know what to do with it."

"What do you mean?"

"Well, my buddy Roger died last night and gave me his Bible. He said his mother had given it to him when he left the States. She had asked him to read it every day and, Chaplain, he sure did. Then, just before he died, he said he wouldn't need it anymore and he gave it to me. He said it helped him a lot and would do the same for me. But I don't know. Maybe I ought to give it to you to give to the patients."

"You keep it. He wanted you to have it."

After observing the power of the Word of God in the hands of the prisoners, Taylor thought he understood better why the Bible had lived through the centuries. "It becomes life itself and lives in the hearts of men," he told himself.

Since there were still twenty-four hundred patients in the hospital, the chaplains organized teams of two or three, often using laymen, to minister to the wards. One would read the New Testament, another would pray, and a third would present some personal testimony or brief devotional thought, and through these personal contacts, hundreds of men were strengthened.

One day while Taylor was working his way through Ward Number Four, which housed the dysentery patients, a young enlisted man named Aaron called him to his bed. He told the chaplain that he heard him preach and now wanted to tell him that he had become a Christian. He had prayed and trusted in the Lord, and now he was happy and confident that, even if he didn't make it, things would be all right.

Aaron's voice was weak, but his words expressed the firm conviction of his heart and soul when he said that now he wanted to partake of the lord's Supper.

"Sure", Aaron, you can take Communion," Taylor replied softly. "I'll make the preparations and be back in about an hour."

Taylor left the boy with mixed feelings, elation that young Aaron had found a new relationship to the Lord, yet unsure he could find bread, wine, grape juice, or even a common substitute to use in Communion.

He walked up and down the compound yard, in and out of wards, looking for something to use but found nothing. Then he walked over to the side of a barracks, sat down on a bamboo bench and silently prayed that God would help him find something to use for the Communion elements.

After sitting quietly for ten or fifteen minutes, Taylor

suddenly became aware of someone standing beside him. He looked up and saw Captain Watanabe.

"Hello, Chaplain Taylor. How are you today?"

Standing and bowing awkwardly, Taylor replied, "Fine, thank you, sir."

"Chaplain Taylor, please come to my office and talk," the captain said. "I need to practice my English."

"Of course, Captain."

Taylor followed the little officer across the parade ground, past the sentry house, to the office of the camp commandant. He remembered he had been there before when he was sentenced to the heat boxes.

"Sit down, Chaplain Taylor."

"Thank you, Captain."

"Oil, ocher mote kite" he barked to a clerk seated at a nearby desk.

Soon the soldier returned carrying a platter with a teapot, some small paper cups and a basket of rice crackers.

"This is Japanese tea, green tea," the captain explained. "And these are rice crackers. We call them somber. Now you eat."

Taylor ate part of his cracker and drank only a portion of the green tea.

"Chaplain Taylor, you do not like Japanese green tea and crackers?"

"Oh yes, I do."

"Then, why you don't eat?"

"Well, I want to save it for later."

"I see. That will be fine."

"Thank you, sir."

"Chaplain Taylor, how long have you been in Cabanatuan?"

"Nearly two and a half years."

"And when the war is over, what will you do?"

"Return to my home in Texas and continue in the ministry."

"Why did you become a chaplain, Mr. Taylor?"

"I felt the call of God to do so."

"It must be wonderful to feel such a call. In the mission school I often heard of such things but had no such experience myself."

"Perhaps someday you will."

"Perhaps. Anyway, let's talk again, Chaplain Taylor."

Taylor bowed again, and carrying the broken somber rice cracker and small amount of green tea in the paper cup, he returned to Ward Number Four and prepared to serve Communion to Aaron.

"The bread signifies the Lord's body which was broken for you, Aaron, for me and all mankind. The Lord said when we eat it to remember his sacrifice for us on the cross," he explained as he handed the rice cracker to the boy.

"The wine told the story of his shed blood, which covers our sins. When we drink it, we think of the fact that his blood was shed to wash away our sins." Taylor placed the edge of the cup between Aaron's lips.

The brightness in Aaron's face remained in Taylor's memory for many days and was a great consolation when the boy died.

On another occasion, Taylor was told that two young men in Ward Twelve wanted to see him. They had been talking about religion for a long time and had decided they would like to become Christians. Would the chaplain help them? One was Jewish, the other, an unbeliever. Yet Taylor saw them both find peace in their hearts.

One by one, Major Takahashi removed the restrictions. Although the prisoners seldom saw him, they knew he was a cheerful little man, completely bald, with a heavy mustache masking a mouth full of yellow, crooked teeth. Horn-rimmed glasses circled his deepset, penetrating eyes. He was an older man, and rumor around the camp had it that he had been a diplomat in Europe and, like Captain Watanabe, spoke excellent English.

Colonel Oliver allowed the new commandant only a few days to get settled before approaching him for permission to build a chapel. When permission was granted, he asked permission to conduct brief worship services for the men who were hospitalized.

"Captain Watanabe tells me you have been doing so anyway and without permission."

"Well, yes, sir. We thought it would help comfort the men."

Takahashi, apparently intent only on establishing his authority, gave the permission.

That same afternoon, the five chaplains began erecting the chapel just north of the hospital. With bolos borrowed from the guards, they split bamboo rails and mounted them on posts.

Benches were made of bamboo logs tied together with scraps of string. The platform, pulpit stand and organ case were made of rattan stems. Of course there was no organ, but Taylor insisted they provide a place for one in case it should show up. A thin layer of banana leaves served as the roof. Nothing more was needed. In a week the chapel was finished.

While rummaging through an old garbage heap near the camp, one of the men found a worn-out typewriter, and he proudly carried it to the chapel.

"Look what I found, Preach."

Taylor looked at it skeptically. The machine was rusted, several keys were missing, and it had no ribbon. Undaunted, the soldier carried the typewriter to his barracks, then went to the commandant's office to request a bottle of ink for use by the chaplains. Then he placed the strips in a small bowl and poured the ink over them, soaking them thoroughly.

It worked. The next morning they had a ribbon, and the soldier started typing up the daily announcements for the chapel bulletin board. Appropriate quotations from the Bible and other bits of news were posted; the missing letters were filled in with pencil.

The chaplains watched as one by one the men sauntered up to the bulletin board and began to read. Long isolated from most books, papers and other channels of information, they reveled in the opportunity to read a wide-awake bulletin board.

"Now the flag," Taylor announced.

"You think it's all right?"

"We'll soon find out."

He cut a thirty-foot bamboo pole and chopped off the branches. Then with the point of a bolo, he made a hole a few inches down from the top, put a piece of cord through it and stretched the cord to the bottom of the pole. As they were digging a hole for the flagpole, a guard wanted to know what they were doing, and Taylor told him that they, too, wanted to have suru. Apparently, the answer satisfied him, for he left them, and shortly after, the pole was in its place.

Father Duffey, when he had been brought to the camp, had not been searched and had managed to bring with him a Christian flag, the symbol of the Chaplain

Corps. Now it was attached to the pulley and slowly raised. As it rippled gently in the breeze over the chapel, Taylor told his friends, ,"I'll never lower it." and the men agreed the Japanese themselves would have to take it if they wanted it.

In one of the wards was a bugler named Ernest Norquest, whom Taylor had known in Bataan. Although he was suffering from a severe leg injury and had to be carried on a stretcher to the chapel, at 5 p.m. he blew the call to church. The bugle had been purchased by a member of a work detail from a Filipino national, and its clarion notes were heard throughout the camp. Within five minutes, the three hundred seats were filled and two hundred more men stood around the chapel.

Dawson led the men in the hymn "A Mighty Fortress Is Our God," read from the Bible, led a prayer, and then introduced Taylor, who said: "Men, two thousand years ago a man went down from Jerusalem to Jericho. Some bandits robbed and beat him and left him for dead. Two men passed by. They just looked at him and kept right on going." As he spoke even the Japanese guards at the edge of the crowd stood in silence.

"Then a Samaritan passed by. He stopped and dressed the wounds, then took the man into town. His example stands today.

Our risen Savior can give us the inner desire to help one another."

His remarks were brief, but every man present felt their power and their message.

Day after day the services continued. The little white cross set in blue flew over the chapel entrance, and the Japanese did not order it taken down. Rather, they looked at it curiously as they passed the chapel until one afternoon, during the five o'clock service a Japanese general's party drove into camp. The general, accompanied by several officers, got out and went toward the group of prisoners standing around the chapel. Carefully he studied the emblem on the flag, then watched the service for a few minutes. A hush settled over the jittery congregation as Taylor addressed the general.

"Sir, we are conducting a religious service. Is there anything you wish?"

The interpreter relayed the question to the stoic-faced general, who presently replied, "Kekko da!" And the interpreter translated, "Proceed with your service."

12.

THE HELL SHIPS

Simultaneous with the American air invasion of the Philippines, the Japanese commander in Manila received orders from Tokyo to begin the evacuation of all American officers from Cabanatuan, O'Donnell and Bilibid.

A gray, steamy overcast enveloped Cabanatuan when, on October 15, 1944, at 3 a.m., the siren in the guard tower split the night, and all the prisoners were ordered to assemble in the yard.

The floodlights from the guard towers blinded Taylor as he stepped from the barracks into the uncertain night.

Major Takahashi marched briskly to the platform in the center of the yard and issued a brief statement that all officers of the American Armed Forces were ordered to Manila for transfer out of the Philippines. They were to leave at 5 a.m. and were to carry only their belongings. As Taylor and Bill Dawson walked back to the barracks, they met Captain Watanabe. "You now leave Cabanatuan," he said to Taylor.

"Yes, in only two hours."

"I will miss you, Chaplain Taylor."

"Thank you, Captain. I hope all goes well with you."

"Oh, have no fear. I will survive."

"Of course."

"You see, Chaplain Taylor, the bamboo is smarter than the oak, for when a typhoon strikes, the bamboo bends before the fierce winds."

"Perhaps someday we will meet again."

"Perhaps."

A kind of sadness, overwhelming because it was not understood, came over Taylor. As he looked at the Japanese captain he experienced deep feelings of sympathy, feelings he would never forget.

It took Taylor only a few minutes to gather his scant belongings: his Bible, toothbrush and change of underwear so he decided to spend his last two hours visiting the hospital, for he knew the hospital would suffer because of the evacuation of the officers. Only a skeletal crew of doctors would remain in Cabanatuan.

Excitement crackled in the ward as he walked up and down the aisles. During the two years he had served in the hospital,

Taylor had become first-name friends to hundreds of the men.

Now his parting seemed unbearable, but as he left each building he said simply, "We don't know what tomorrow holds, but we know the one who holds tomorrow. We face an uncertain future and may never meet again here on this earth, but we can be sure we'll meet again in heaven. No one, not even the Japanese, not even death itself, can take that from us."

Then he led each group in the Lord's Prayer and walked sadly away.

Exactly at 5 a.m., a convoy of Japanese Toyota trucks entered Cabanatuan to pick up the two thousand officers ordered to Japan as hostages.

As Taylor and Dawson prepared to board one of the lead trucks they saw Colonel Oliver approaching.

"Come on, Colonel, climb aboard," Dawson said.

"I'm not going. Zerphas and I are staying."

"Not going? What do you mean, not going?" Taylor asked.

"We're staying with the enlisted men."

"But Takahashi said all officers ."

"I know, but I spoke with him and he's allowing Zerph and me and three doctors to stay here and I'll be all right."

"We'll miss you, Colonel," Taylor said.

"Take care of yourself," added Dawson.

"God go with you, boys, and remember, keep looking up, there'll be a brighter day tomorrow."

Taylor could not adequately express his deep feelings for the chaplain, who had been like a father to the younger ones.

Although they were saddened at the thought of leaving him behind, they were thankful he would be spared the uncertain journey.

When the trucks were full they chugged out the gate. For some, the ride to Manila was an unexpected time of excitement and release from the routine of camp imprisonment. For others, it was only a hated factor of further uncertainty.

Just before noon the trucks drove through the steel gates of Bilibid. As Taylor jumped down from the truck, he looked at the foreboding walls and thought the place had changed little during the two and a half years.

Guards divided the prisoners into groups of fifty and marched them to several makeshift buildings that had concrete floors.

Taylor soon discovered the food situation was far worse than it had been in Cabanatuan, for it consisted only of camotes and a small portion of rice served twice daily, and morale plummeted to a new low. But then renewed courage followed each American bombing raid on Nichols Field and other Japanese military installations in and around Manila Bay. Deep in his heart, Taylor believed he could endure the starvation for a while and prayed fervently that the prison might be liberated before the prisoners were forced to embark for Japan.

From mid-October to mid-December the chaplains: Father Duffey, Dawson, Taylor, and Art Cleveland, who had come in from O'Donnell, conducted regular worship services for the men in Bilibid and ministered personally to the sick in the hospital area, three tents near the south wall. Some of the members of the Cabanatuan choir, including Major Shurtz, assisted with the worship services.

The chapel altar and pulpit were installed against the dark-gray wall which had enclosed the death chamber of the old Spanish prison. A small roof covered them, and planks, nailed to tops of posts, formed seats for the worshipers. Each evening at six, devotional services were held, and the chaplains conducted services Sunday morning and evening as well.

After two months in Bilibid, sixteen hundred officers were alerted for a journey to the Japanese mainland, but Taylor knew the possibility of successfully making the sea voyage was remote. American planes had been operating over the Philippine Islands and South China Sea for three months and had destroyed everything that moved in and out of Manila Bay. But the Japanese command was frantic. American landing parties had assaulted Leyte and had moved to within two hundred miles of Manila. The American officers had to be moved to Ja-pan, and late in the evening of December 12, the guards notified the detail scheduled for transfer to Japan. The POW ship, they announced, would sail the next morning.

Although it was expected, the announcement came as a shock and disappointment to Taylor. For weeks he had hoped the bombings and the American forces moving on Manila would force the Japanese to abandon their plan.

That night no one slept. The officers spent the time writing letters to their families and visiting with buddies not scheduled to sail.

Taylor learned that besides Bill Dawson, Father Duffey, and Art Cleveland, and eleven other chaplains from O'Donnell and Bilibid would be on board.

About midnight, the chaplains from Cabanatuan met outside the entrance to the makeshift hospital.

"We've come a long way, men," Taylor said. "And tomorrow is another day."

"It's already been a long journey," Dawson said. "But I've never felt more at peace and a greater sense of fulfillment in my life. If I had it all to do over again, I wouldn't change."

"We've shown the whole world what God can do," Father Duffey added. "The miracle in the hearts of the men of Cabanatuan will be a hallmark in the story of men imprisoned."

Taylor also bid farewell to Colonel Johnson and Drs. North and Schwartz. He wondered if he would ever see them again.

The night was long, and the men milled around restlessly.

They had endured three years of prison life, and now, at a time when liberation seemed imminent, they had been ordered to prepare for a hazardous sea voyage.

At ten o'clock the following morning, sixteen hundred officers stood in marching formation facing the main prison gate. They were ready when the Japanese commander ordered them to begin the march to the ship, and the ragtag army moved through the steel gates toward the port of Manila.

As Taylor walked through the city, he could see all the evidences of war and hardship. The once-beautiful parks and playgrounds around the walled city Lunetta had been converted into vegetable gardens, and there were shell holes where streets used to be. He saw smashed buildings and burned-out battle equipment, and everywhere were signs of impoverishment, starvation and wretchedness among the few civilians who ventured out to see the prisoners pass.

The column approached the street which led across Quezon Bridge and then to Pier Seven. There Taylor felt the cooling breeze as he looked out over the bay. All across the bay, particularly in the direction of Cavite and Corregidor, hulls of destroyed ships were silent monuments to the effectiveness of the American air power.

A number of Japanese ships lined the pier, and Taylor noticed each ship had Maru following its name. He was told it was the equivalent to the SS prefix of American ships.

Most of the troop carriers were old hulks bought from the United States during the Depression, but one of the ships was different. It was the Oraoka Maru, the one to which Taylor's group had been assigned. As he looked at it, he judged it to be about 5o,ooo tons, maybe more. He heard it had been a first-class luxury liner prior to the war, and it was still a beautiful ship with all conveniences and up-to-date equipment. The presence of women and children on board gave it the air of a holiday ship. Apparently, due to the threat of the invasion of Manila by American ground forces, the officers' and diplomats' families were being returned to the mainland.

Late in the afternoon the order was given to board ship, and within two hours 1620 prisoners were on deck. Then they were ordered into the holds, about 800 aft, 600 fore, and 220 amidships. The guards ordered the prisoners to march single file. When Taylor reached the entrance, he looked through the hatch, and what he saw in the aft hold of the ship made him forget all the accumulated miseries of the past. It was indescribable horror and madness. At first he thought the Japanese were trying to get all 1620 prisoners into the foul-smelling aft hold that measured only 50 by 70 feet.

All the space in the hold was filled, yet the guards kept forcing men through the hatch. A guard shoved Taylor in, and he came face to face with men who looked like ghosts. They reminded him of a frightened deer he had once seen in East Texas when he was a boy. Each man was soaked in perspiration.

The holds of the Oraoka Maru were without any ventilation, and the heat was indescribable. Many of the men fainted from heatstroke and suffocation. Some of those who fainted fell to the floor and were trampled to death by the other prisoners. Others were suffering convulsions and seemed to be dying.

As usual, the Japanese were disorganized. They had miscalculated the number of prisoners they would be transporting and looked almost insane when they discovered they could not get all the men into the holds.

Some of the unconscious men were picked up and moved by hand over the heads of the other prisoners to the hatch, then carried to the deck. There, several were revived and immediately ordered back into the hold.

Taylor had heard of the Black Hole of Calcutta, where the rising tide would drown the British prisoners, but he couldn't imagine it any worse than the hold of the Oraoka Maru.

Compounding the situation was the lack of sanitation facilities.

There were only two latrines, one on each side of the top deck, and it was obvious they could not accommodate 1620 men.

Urinations, due to dehydration, were abnormally frequent, and to reach the latrine a prisoner had to walk over his buddies, some sitting, some standing, then climb out the hatch to the deck. Some were too weak even to try, and at times the guards pushed others back down the steel ladder.

When the situation became unbearable, the guards provided two washtubs which were placed in the aft hold. These were intended for the dysentery cases. It helped some, but the stench made those nearby vomit.

Taylor reckoned the space allotted to each ten men in the hold to be about four by six feet, and it was worse than the heat boxes at Cabanatuan. He had never felt so miserable in his life, for December in the Philippines is very hot and one of the driest months.

At sunset the Oraoka Maru sailed out of Manila Bay, passed Bataan and Corregidor, and headed up the eastern coast of the Philippines. But even at sea the heat continued. The prisoners soon consumed the contents of their canteens, and when daylight came, Taylor heard, by count, that thirty men had died during the night in the aft hold. The bodies were moved by hand over the heads of other prisoners and raised to the deck.

Taylor, too, made his way through the men to the ladder, climbed to the top and pounded on the hatch. A guard yelled, "Dame zo," and Taylor shouted back, "I ask for permission to conduct a Christian funeral." There was no answer. Uncere- moniously, the Japanese dropped the bodies into the sea.

About midmorning, Taylor heard the drone of planes approaching the convoy. Guns from the Oraoka Maru began firing, and the repercussion shook the entire ship. Seconds later, bombs began falling on all the ships except the Oraoka. They were all destroyed. Then the bombing ceased.

Late in the afternoon the Japanese evacuated all women and children from the ship, leaving only the prisoners in the holds and a few guards.

During the evening the ship was moved into Subic Bay and anchored four hundred yards from shore.

The tropical sun disappeared below the horizon, but the darkness brought little relief for the men sweltering in the hold,.

When the Oraoka stopped, all movement and air circulation ceased, and they became steaming infernos.

Meanwhile, the Japanese guards, who had been left behind to watch the prisoners, deserted the ship, leaving no water to quench the prisoners' gnawing thirst. Nor did they provide for ventilation.

Another thirty men died during the night. Ten others committed suicide. Taylor recognized physical hardships as only a part of the problem. Fear and panic were beginning to sweep through the hold. From time to time the men became an uncontrollable mob, screaming and pounding against the sides of the ship. Then the noise subsided, and all that could be heard was the water gurgling against the ship. Taylor knew that even an animal can't be thus confined for long without going mad.

About midnight, Lieutenant Wada, the interpreter, opened the hatch and told the prisoners that at daybreak they would be allowed to leave ship by boat for the beach. The hatch was then quickly closed, but all the men felt a little relief from the small amount of air that had circulated through the hold.

His promise proved empty words. Daybreak came, but nothing happened until 8:45 a.m., when Taylor again heard the roar of American planes and suddenly realized what was happening. The purpose of the evacuation delay was clear. The prisoners on board the Oraoka were to remain on the ship to pay with their own lives for the losses inflicted on the other ships of the Japanese convoy.

The roar of the dive bombers became ear-splitting as they came closer and closer. Then, having no idea that American prisoners were locked in the holds, the American pilots bombed the ship repeatedly.

A direct hit cut a wide gash in the aft deck, spraying the prisoners with hot shrapnel. A piece hit Taylor in the right arm, causing his hand to become numb; another hit his hip, and he almost lost consciousness. Unable to move, barely able to breathe, he prayed, "Lord, are we finished? Show us, Lord." And as his lips moved in prayer, the officers near him also began to pray. Their delirium faded and their hearts focused on hope that God might yet spare them.

"Lord, let us go down or get us out of here. But let us not die like dogs." Taylor prayed, barely audibly. Then he lapsed into complete unconsciousness.

When the smoke cleared, the hole in the deck above was visible and the men began crawling through it. Taylor came to and helped the men climb to the deck. Hurriedly, others made their way up the rope ladders to the hatch and tried to force it open.

The aft hold began to empty. Some, still inside, walked around like stunned animals, and Taylor led several to the open hole, urging them to climb to the top. Then he examined the men sprawled on the floor and counted two hundred dead, their mangled bodies in various stages of disfigurement.

He turned toward the open hole and almost stumbled over a lifeless form next to the side of the ship. Looking down, he recognized the body of Major Shurtz. Squatting down, he cradled his head in his arms and prayed, "Dear God, receive this faithful man into your kingdom."

Then Taylor felt the ship listing, said a last good-bye to Shurtz, and using only his left arm crawled through the hole up onto the deck.

Within minutes, hundreds of men had jumped into the water and were swimming toward shore. There were no small boats or life vests, and many of them, weak from exhaustion and starvation, were overcome by the waves.

Still, the American dive bombers circled and began another approach on the badly damaged vessel. The men in the water waved their hands frantically, trying to get the attention of the pilots, and finally one plane broke formation and came in at low altitude just above the waves. The pilot realized the men in the water were Americans and dipped his wings in confirmation.

The squadron withdrew and, with the dive bombers gone, the prisoners who had remained on ship jumped into the water and swam toward the beach, about four hundred yards away. Before leaving the ship, Taylor made a quick check of the middle and forward holds. Men lay everywhere, some without limbs, others still moaning, still others delirious, screaming.

Taylor counted four hundred more bodies, and he stopped to pray, "Take unto thyself, dear Lord, the souls of the valiant.

Some there be which have no sepulcher, their name liveth for evermore. Oh Lord, support us all day long until the shadows lengthen and our work is done. Then, in thy mercy, grant us a safe lodging and a holy rest and place at the last." When he had finished the Seaman's Prayer, he jumped into the water and swam toward shore.

As Taylor neared the beach, suddenly and without warning, the Japanese guards began firing at the men in the water. Men's heads began bobbing in and out of the water as they tried to dodge the bullets and at the same time keep from drowning.

When he could hold his breath no longer, Taylor came out of the water for a breath of air. Then fear from the sound of the cracking rifles on the beach sent him under again. Frantically he tried to stay afloat among the floundering men. A few feet away he saw Chaplain Cleveland bobbing up and down in the water. Then he went down and didn't come up. Two men nearby dove and brought him up. They tried to keep the injured chaplain from drowning and at the same time dodge the Japanese rifle fire from the beach, but as Taylor made his way toward Cleveland he suddenly saw him wince in pain and roll over in the water. He had taken a direct hit in the head. The two men supporting him swam away and continued their fight for survival.

Even as he attempted to rub the burning salt water from his bloodshot eyes, Taylor, in a fleeting moment, remembered with intense admiration the tall, likable Cleveland, the Disciples minister from the Midwest, a personal friend.

Slowly he made his way toward the spot where Cleveland drowned, said a brief prayer, then realized his friend was gone forever.

The guards continued firing, killing another hundred and fifty men before their guns ceased and the prisoners swam the last fifty yards to the beach, lifted their hands in surrender, and joined the other prisoners on four old tennis courts a few hundred feet from Subic Bay.

Taylor saw Bill Dawson and Father Duffey and walked over to where they sat to tell them the bad news about Major Shurtz and Art Cleveland.

Again Taylor heard the drone of the American planes. Flying out of the sun, the planes came in for a reconnaissance of the listing ship, and after determining that no Americans were on board, made several direct hits. In a few minutes the ship sank leaving only a heavy oil smudge low on the horizon. When the prisoners cheered, it so infuriated the guards that they began wholesale mistreatment of the men, kicking, shoving and hitting them with their rifle butts.

For six days the guards confined the prisoners to the tennis courts. They were fed nothing except on the fourth day, when they brought a sixty-pound bag of uncooked rice and distributed it to the starving men, about three tablespoons each.

Nearly all the men had lost their clothing except for their shorts. During the daytime the tropical sun burned their unprotected skin. At night they shivered from the chilly breezes from Subic Bay.

Meanwhile, the doctors performed a dozen operations and were able to save some of the wounded men. But there were no sharp instruments or anesthetics, the guards refused to help, and a great many died. They were given Christian burial on the sandy beach.

On December 22, six days later, the guards brought trucks to remove the prisoners. The medical officers appealed to the commander to return the wounded men to the hospital at Cabanatuan, but the Japanese commander flatly refused.

"Then, let us take the worst cases to the hospital," Dr. Gregg requested.

"Sore wa kekko da," the commander agreed. He ordered the doctor to pick twenty men for transfer, and these, many of them unconscious, were loaded into the trucks. But Taylor had an ominous feeling as the trucks drove away that the helpless men would never be heard from again.

More than a thousand men were loaded into the other trucks and transferred to San Fernando Pampanga, where they bivouacked around the grounds of the city jail for two nights. Then, on Christmas Eve, 1944, they were marched to the city railroad depot. At 8 a.m. the following morning, at the very time when American planes could be seen bombing nearby Clark Field and other Japanese installations, the train pulled out of San Fernando.

Japanese guards continued to create bizarre methods for dealing with the prisoners. At the first stop the interpreter opened the door to the car where Taylor was and ordered two dozen men out, forcing them to climb the steel ladder on the side of the old boxcar to the top.

There they were forced to sit down for the remainder of the trip as protection against American planes.

Except for several other stops to take on fuel, the tiny freight train traveled steadily north, and late the following night it arrived in the city of San Fernando La Union, where the prisoners immediately detrained on the beaches of Lingayen Gulf. The Japanese stretched barbed wire at angles to the water and ordered the prisoners inside, where they sat until daybreak.

Christmas Day had passed.

At sunrise the guards ordered the men to form columns of two and marched them through La Union five miles over a gravel road that tore at their bare feet. Then, when they were well into the country they bivouacked near a little country school building. Another strand of barbed wire was strung around the area.

Medics asked for volunteers to carry the men with the highest fever and worst dysentery into the schoolhouse. Taylor, Dawson and Father Duffey helped four litter details carry the sick into the building, where they would be in the shade. The other men lay down on the grass.

At noon the guards brought water and several barrels of strained rice. One of the American officers asked Taylor to lead in prayer, and he walked to the center of the wire enclosure and invited the men to bow their heads.

"Father in heaven, at this Christmastime, we find ourselves in a hostile place in the hands of cruel taskmasters. We are beaten without cause, mistreated without reason, and starved without concern. But for this small portion of food we are still grateful.

We thank you for it. Today, once again, we commit ourselves to thee, and whether it be by life or by death, all that we are is thine. We pray for our families and loved ones in the States.

May the true spirit of Christmas be theirs, and may they never know the blackness of this hour. In Jesus' name, amen."

In less than one minute the food was gone. No one knew but what it would be their last meal but, once eaten, it was theirs.

No one could take it from them.

A dull, monotonous afternoon turned into a dull, monotonous evening. But to the prisoners' surprise, just before sunset the guards ordered them into formation and marched them out of the camp. Again the sharp gravel, protruding from the country road, tore at the men's bare feet. Taylor recognized the terrain as that over which they had marched during the morning. When they arrived in La Union, an interpreter told them, "Tomorrow you sail Japan. Tonight you sleep here."

After a sleepless night, Taylor joined the vigil to spot the first ship. Bill Dawson and Father Duffey, who had been further back in the column, joined him.

"What do you think?" Duffey asked.

"I don't know and I don't think they do," Taylor replied.

"One thing's for sure," Dawson said. "If we don't get relief soon, we're all dead."

All day they waited, yet no ships were sighted. Taylor asked permission for the prisoners to move off the hot sand to the palm trees, but the request was denied, and by afternoon some of the men began to collapse on the burning sand. Dr. Gregg asked the guard for water but was told none was available. Then an officer stepped out from among the prisoners.

"Yes, there is water about a hundred and fifty yards from the beach," he said.

The guards argued back and forth among themselves, then shoving their bayonets up against the man's ribs, they motioned for him to lead them to the water,

Taylor did not know the officer's name and was afraid he would never see him again, but in a short time he returned and the guards began bringing buckets of water to the men.

Taylor later learned that the officer had once been stationed near La Union and knew the area well.

The prisoners slept on the sandy beaches until 2 a.m.. Then the guards began shouting for them to form columns of two, and a bowlegged guard, his samurai sword clanking against his high, brown leather boots, led the way toward a nearby pier which extended out to an anchored ship.

On the way down the pier, a young boy beside Taylor fell down. Taylor picked him up and, with the help of Bill Dawson, carried him to the side of the ship. There they waited their turn to climb a rope ladder to the deck. An officer in a white uniform, holding a megaphone in his hand, glared at the two chaplains as they helped the boy up the ladder. "Hayaku! Hayaku! Hayaku!" he yelled through the megaphone, hurrying the men up the rope.

Japanese sailors lined the deck but refused to look directly at the prisoners. Taylor knew this was typically oriental, an attitude of complete impersonality toward their captives.

Meanwhile, the sailors were already taking the hawsers from the posts on the pier prior to weighing anchor.

Feeling like a galley slave, Taylor surveyed the old,

grimy ship, searching for some kind of identification. It was a weather-beaten vessel, apparently used only in times of emergency, and he reckoned it to be a 10,000-ton freighter.

As he slowly made his way up the gangplank, following Bill Dawson toward the forward hold, he was stopped by a guard.

Dawson was the last man allowed fore. Taylor was ordered aft, so the two friends were separated.

The gray freighter sailed out of Lingayen Gulf, north toward Japan, its holds crowded far beyond capacity. Within an hour, men began fainting from heat exhaustion. There was no room for movement, and once a prisoner sat down, he could not get up. Men had to take turns changing positions. Those who had been sitting for an hour stood up to give those standing a chance to sit. It helped alleviate the cramps that came from being forced to stay in rigid positions.

Taylor cringed at the thought of how impersonal everything had become. No man dared venture to ask the next his name.

Although there were still acts of selflessness, with each passing hour the men became more and more intent on personal survival amid the stench of inhuman conditions.

At noon the next day the hatch opened and the interpreter ordered the prisoners to hand the dead out the hatch. The bodies were lifted to the top deck, and the guard quickly dropped them over the side of the ship into the water. It made a little more breathing space in the hold, but Taylor regretted the men had no Christian burial. Silently he prayed God to have mercy on their souls.

A while later, a guard brought water, about half a canteen per man, provided the man could get to it. Another brought rice in filthy wooden buckets. Taylor was so famished he couldn't swallow the pasty stuff. When the ship sailed out into the rough China Sea, the prisoners became seasick with the pitch and roll of the ship. One man went insane and started screaming. Others had to be bound and gagged to keep from harming themselves or trying to commit suicide. More severe cases of dysentery developed, but each time a doctor protested the conditions, he received an abusive reply from the captain, who stayed drunk most of the time. Finally, seeing that the latrines were overflowing, a guard signaled to the prisoners that that they could come on deck to use another makeshift latrine. But the new freedom created other problems. The stairway to the latrine passed a guards' quarters, and any disturbance, no matter how minor, provoked the Japanese so that they rushed out to beat and kick the prisoners as they passed by.

Taylor noticed the men were becoming cowed and fearful of the Japanese. For months they had maintained their dignity despite beatings and other abuses, but now they were losing their will to survive. For three years they had been obstinate, willing to fight, clinging to individual freedom and dignity, but the events of the past few days and the confinement in the holds of the ship had broken their will. Some whimpered when they were beaten. Some begged.

After four days and nights, the ship dropped anchor in Techow Harbor, Formosa, and those who could see through the open hatch reported signs of heavy American bombings everywhere.

Taylor hoped the ship would proceed on to Japan immediately, but his hope was short-lived. The interpreter told the prisoners they would be in Techow indefinitely.

There was very little conversation in the hold. The whole world seemed to have turned to madness, without compassion.

Even the chaplains no longer had the energy to conduct devotionals of any kind, barely enough to pray. Food rations dwindled, since the guards claimed no food was available on Formosa, and on January 13, when the ships once again weighed anchor and sailed toward Japan, conditions worsened. Men died by the hundreds, and the living lost even the energy necessary for complaints.

Then, six days out of Formosa, Taylor again heard the drone of American dive bombers. This time the forward hold took a direct hit. There were no survivors. Bill Dawson, and a hundred more, were killed by American planes. When it was discovered that the ship was listing, the prisoners were ordered to the deck.

"Bill's gone," Taylor told Father Duffey as he stepped off the ladder. The Catholic chaplain's face dropped, and he bowed his head. Then he crossed himself, and in one of the most reverent actions Taylor ever witnessed, Father Duffey dropped to his knees in prayer for his lost friend. All through the night Taylor kept remembering that only one number, one gesture from a Japanese guard, diverting him from the fore hold, kept him from dying with Bill Dawson.

The second day after the bombing, a Japanese medical team from another ship, accompanied by a group of photographers, boarded the half-sunken ship. They provided routine first aid for the slightly wounded in the middle and aft holds, but they did not visit the fore hold. The Americans who remained on deck speculated that the medical team had come only to make propaganda pictures on how well their medical corps cared for wounded prisoners of war, for they took their pictures and left, leaving the American doctors in the holds helpless with no bandages, medicines or equipment and dependent on improvisation by every possible means.

By chance, it was discovered the Japanese had stored several tons of sugar on the bottom deck, and Taylor asked the commanding officer for permission to bring some to the wounded, starving men.

Through the interpreter, the commander replied that any American prisoner found with sugar would be severely punished. Nevertheless, during the night, while the guards slept, several men slipped below and brought the sugar to the wounded.

The next day the Japanese commander, discovering part of the sugar supply missing, ordered an investigation. When no evidence was found, he ordered the guilty prisoners to identify themselves or mass punishment would be inflicted on all. However, when the men heard the nature of the punishment, no one stepped forward. The commander threatened to cut the daily ration of the pasty rice. No one cared, especially since the energy gained from the sweet sugar more than compensated for the discontinued portions of rice.

The small portion of sugar had lifted Taylor's spirits to the point where he began feeling guilty about not conducting any kind of religious services, and he told Father Duffey that perhaps they should try to have devotions. When the priest agreed, Taylor stepped to the center of the hold and quoted a familiar passage of

Scripture. Then he offered a brief prayer. There was little response just a wink here, a nod there, a gentle smile.

Disappointed, Taylor returned to the rear of the hold, but Father Duffey consoled him: "It's okay, Preston. They're too far gone to feel anything."

On the afternoon of January 20, the prisoners were ordered to prepare for transfer from the listing vessel to another prison ship and, as Taylor stepped out of the hatch he looked again at the forward hold, which still entombed his closest friend. He prayed God to receive the souls of all the dead and be merciful to them in the future life.

Moving the remaining six hundred and fifty prisoners to the other ship proved a task far beyond the guards' expectation.

Most of the men were wounded, and the rest were so starved they didn't have the strength to climb the rope ladders.

Some of the guards began assisting them, and Taylor reflected that it was the first kind act he had seen on the part of the Japanese in weeks.

This time the prisoners were herded into a small hold near the top deck of the old seagoing vessel. They were transferred to a ship they soon realized had previously been used to transport cattle. The floor was ankle-deep in cow manure and infested with lice.

At midnight another explosion awakened Taylor from half sleep. He thought the ship had been hit by a torpedo or a bomb, for it rocked under the terrific impact. The men panicked and rushed toward the hatch, but they were turned back by guards with submachine guns and hand grenades dangling from leather straps around their necks. The sky was red with flames of burning ships.

Taylor felt like a rat in a trap. He heard other prisoners threaten to rush the guards to escape, but he knew it would be certain death for every man in the hold. Nevertheless, many men were willing to take the risk and, as the agitation increased, the prisoners soon became a howling mob.

Taylor pushed his way to the center of the hold, bowed his head, and began saying the Lord's Prayer. Gradually the din subsided and the prisoners joined him in reciting the prayer.

Later, they learned there had been no explosion at all. The prison ship had struck another ship in the convoy, and both had caught fire. In a few hours the flames were brought under control.

The Japanese, Taylor discovered, though apparently stoic, were very excitable. Prior to dropping depth charges, they yelled and screamed orders with staccato bursts of their monosyllabic language, then repeated themselves over and over. Taylor had difficulty understanding their apparent presence of mind even in the face of impending disaster, contrasted with the excited yells and actions which accompanied the giving of orders.

As the convoy neared Moji, Japan, without warning the weather turned cold, intensely cold. Snow and ice covered the decks. In the tropics the prisoners had suffered from the heat; now dressed only in shorts, they huddled together trying to keep warm, and they managed to steal sugar sacks from the lower deck to fashion blankets from the crude cloth.

Daily food rations dwindled to one cup of rice for four men; other days they received no food at all. But worst of all was the thirst. One day Taylor saw a West

Point man trade his class ring to a guard for a cupful of water. Men went insane or committed suicide. Scores of men died daily.

Still, Father Duffey and Taylor took turns conducting the devotionals. There were also a number of men who wanted personal counsel, men who had never embraced Christianity and now wanted to do so.

One professed unbeliever told Taylor, "I've been wrong about you Christians. You really are different. You haven't preached to me, only tried to love me, and I've decided to follow your advice and receive Christ into my heart."

After each day's time of inspiration, Taylor went to where Colonel Gregg lay and asked, "How do you feel, Doctor?" The heroic doctor from Cabanatuan would only smile faintly and try to move his lips. He seemed to have lost the will to live, and Taylor knew he couldn't last much longer.

Father Duffey mentioned that the Japanese had set up a sort of miniature sick bay on the fore deck, ostensibly to care for the worst cases, and they decided Taylor should approach the guard and ask for permission to take Gregg to the sick bay. The guard called the interpreter, who glanced at the men in the hold, their greasy, wet arms and legs all entangled like a bunch of snakes and said, "Okay. You bring doctor."

Taylor bowed politely and returned to the hold to help Father Duffey lift the doctor up the steel ladder to the fore deck. When they arrived at the sick bay, the orderly in charge noticed Taylor's arm infection and said, "You need attention also. You stay."

Taylor lay down on the bunk beside Dr. Gregg, who was beginning to stir. "How do you feel?" Taylor asked.

"Well, you know."

"You got to hang in there, Doc."

"There's no need to fight it anymore."

"Doctor, don't talk like that. You can make it."

"No, there's no way to fight it any longer."

He turned his face away from Taylor and suddenly was gone.

"Oh my God, help this good man."

Even as Taylor prayed, he remembered the day in Cabanatuan when Gregg had accepted responsibility for the escape of a man, then was spared miraculously by the commandant. He knew the doctor had not been born to be a hero. Circumstances forced it upon him. And he received it well.

Father Duffey requested a Christian burial for Gregg and the twelve other men who had died during the night, and when, to his surprise, the request was granted, they wrapped the thirteen bodies in sugar sacks and carried them to the deck, laying them out in a straight row. The guards wouldn't come near the POWs, dressed only in their shorts in the biting wind.

Softly Duffey knelt and placed his hand on the sack in which the body of Dr. Gregg was wrapped.

"God, we commit them to the deep. We yearn for the day when the sea will give up the dead and there will be no more death, nor suffering, nor tears. Their souls we commit to thee.

We know no other but thee. God be merciful to us all, amen." One by one the bodies splashed into the freezing waters.

13.

FUKUOKA 22

The next morning, January30, 1945, the convoy arrived in Moji, Japan, a major port and industrial center on the Shimonoseki Strait.

Guards ordered the POWs still able to stand to bring the dead and the unconscious on deck, and soon thereafter a Japanese general and his party walked up the gangplank and conducted an inspection while two aides took copious notes.

At exactly 10 a. m., the prisoners were ordered to disembark, and those who could walk were herded down the gangway to run a gauntlet of men in white coats spraying disinfectants on them. The fierce, biting wind chilled Taylor till his teeth chattered. He was barefoot, and after walking only a short distance through the snow, his feet numbed. As the column headed down the street, men, women and children came from everywhere, yet kept their distance. These people, who had used manure for centuries to fertilize their gardens, now held their noses as the prisoners passed by. The guards led the columns eight blocks across Moji to an old assembly hall. Then volunteers were requested to return to the ships to bring the wounded.

"Why couldn't we have brought them with us in the first place?" Father Duffey asked.

"Typical Jap planning," Taylor replied.

However, both chaplains volunteered, and by mid-afternoon the prisoners, many unconscious, were carried on makeshift litter to the town assembly hall.

Once inside the hall the men had plenty of breathing room, but there were no fires and the intense cold forced them to huddle together in small groups on the concrete floor. During the afternoon a score of other prisoners died while awaiting transfer from the building.

At 3 p.m., members of the Japanese Red Cross arrived with small baskets of rice and a little fish. Some of the prisoners enjoyed it, but others were too weak to eat.

As Taylor looked over the huddled groups of men, he counted four hundred of the sixteen hundred who had left Cabanatuan. Slowly he ate the fish and rice and then began visiting separate groups to try to piece together bits of information about his chaplain friends. When he learned that twelve of the fourteen chaplains had died on the ships, he tried to cry, but no tears came as he finally realized that he and Father Duffey were the only surviving chaplains.

Three hours later the guards split the prisoners into smaller details and loaded them into olive-colored Toyota trucks for transfer to various work camps scattered throughout Kyushu, Japan's southernmost island.

One hundred ten POWs, including Taylor with his useless left arm, were loaded into army ambulances for transfer to the Moji hospital. Father Duffey stuck his head in the back of Taylor's ambulance to say, "Hang in there, Preston. I'll see you back in Fort Worth when this mess is over."

"It's a deal, Duff," Taylor replied.

The patients had been told the hospital was staffed

by American doctors and were greatly disappointed when Japanese doctors appeared.

The hospital wards, small wooden structures, were unheated. Grass mats on the floor substituted for beds, but each man was given several wool blankets, and for the first time in days they were warm.

Outside, sleet and snow beat against the wooden buildings. Inside, the prisoners covered themselves completely, head to foot, and dared not peek outside the covers for fear they might lose their hold on the warmth.

Twice a day, hospital attendants brought rations, fish and rice, but even so, within eight days after being admitted to the Moji hospital, seventy of the one hundred and ten officers died. Each day, Taylor pulled himself out from under the wool blankets and walked naked, except for his underwear, into the bitter cold to say words over the dead men before returning to his grass mat.

For the first time, Taylor discovered he hated the Japanese and it bothered him. For days the Japanese doctors had observed the sick men in the hospital, yet had done nothing to help. Taylor thought that Jesus of Nazareth must have suffered more than he did, yet Jesus loved and prayed for his persecutors. Then he realized a difference – Jesus was God, he was a man – and he prayed, "Help me to be more like Jesus, less like Preston Taylor."

Love is of people, by people and for people, Taylor reminded himself. Things are to be used; people are to be loved. It is immoral when people are used and things are loved. He also knew that works of hate have ways of surprising their creators, taking on a life of their own that cannot be predicted or controlled.

Each evening, Taylor went to the two wards and conducted devotional services for the remaining forty men. They were anxious in mind, receptive in heart, and participated freely in worship. There were no Bibles, prayer books or hymnals, but he repeated a Scripture verse several times until they could all say it together. A final prayer closed each brief encounter.

On February 25, the forty surviving patients were transferred by ambulance to Fukuoka 22, a prison camp a few miles from the city that held several hundred Australian POWs. The hospital patients were the only American in the camp.

As the ambulances drove through the gate, Taylor noticed the camp buildings were gray stucco, made from the black Japanese earth mixed with a dab of cement. Double-deck stalls lined each side of the buildings, leaving narrow passageways down the middle. The lower bunks were only two feet above the floor, and Taylor soon discovered that the wind whistled at is passed through the crevices of the old buildings.

At either end of the building there was a fat, green Japanese hibachi for burning charcoal, but since there was no charcoal, they served only as ornaments.

The Australians received the sick and wounded Americans with enthusiasm and kindness. On the night the prisoners arrived in camp, the Aussies prepared a supper of fish, rice and coffee, the first coffee Taylor had drink in more than three years.

Captain Moore, the dapper, ranking officer in the camp, immediately recognized the seriousness of the Americans' condition, and appealed to the Japanese hospital for help. Two days later, all the American prisoners were admitted.

"Heat, bloody heat, it's great!" Captain Moore told

Taylor, as they walked toward the hospital. "And have no doubt about it. My lads won't stand for any more hard stuff on you Joes. We'll see damn well to that."

Taylor and Captain Moore became fast friends. Each day, the little officer from New South Wales visited him to discuss the war and the possibility of its conclusion. Taylor immediately recognized him as an intelligent man, quiet and confident.

"I reminded the bloke who runs this place that we're buddies, you and me," he said to Taylor one day. "One Aussie against a hundred Nips, that puts the odds in our favor, I'd say." Taylor could only smile and thank God for those who could still laugh.

The little captain's cheerfulness was infectious, and soon he had the American prisoners laughing and joking with him.

Taylor felt much better. The Japanese doctor dressed his arm, and both it and his hip began to heal. In a month he was released from the hospital, along with many other patients, leaving only the most serious cases. Upon dismissal from the hospital, the POWs received warm clothing and bedding.

One evening the Japanese commander, captain Konno, summoned Taylor to his headquarters. The guard ordered him to remove his shoes before stepping into the room where the commander, dressed in a dark-blue yukata and also barefoot, waited.

Komban wa, Chaplain Taylor."

"Good evening."

"Chaplain Taylor, you are better now?"

"Much better, thank you."

"Japanese Government sorry you are ill so long. Accept humble apology."

"Taylor bowed slightly.

"You are brave man, Chaplain Taylor."

"Only ordinary, Captain Konno."

"Courage is the first of human qualities, for it is the quality which guarantees all others. Churchill said that." The captain grinned.

"I'm not a man of courage, captain. Many times I've been afraid – of pain, sickness, hunger."

"And death?"

"Never death."

"Oh?"

"Death is easy. Living is difficult."

"You Christians are amazing. No fear of death. You are a brave man, Chaplain Taylor. A brave man dies only once, a coward dies a thousand times."

Taylor had known some brave men – on Bataan, in Cabanatuan, on the hell ships. Bill Dawson, Major Shurtz and a thousand others. However, somehow he had never thought of himself as being brave.

"But the history-makers, Chaplain Taylor, are not brave men but the power structures of the conquerors. But alas, our day has come and your troops stand at our door."

"And what will you do, captain?"

"I return to my students at the Imperial University. And I hope soon."

"I hope so, too."

For a long moment captain Konno started at the frail, emaciated chaplain, then said, "Chaplain Taylor, why you no request permission to conduct memorial service for your president?

"Our president?"

"Yes, Chaplain Taylor, your president he die two

weeks ago."

"Captain, we did not know."

"I think, Chaplain Taylor, your president a great leader, maybe world's greatest leader. You will conduct a memorial service to honor Mr. Roosevelt?"

"Yes, of course."

On the following evening, at 6 p.m., the Americans, joined by Captain Moore and a group of Australian enlisted men, gathered in the camp yard for the memorial service to President Roosevelt.

With the permission of the commandant, Taylor led the men in singing "America the Beautiful," and the Australians, much moved, listened to the forty Americans sing.

As strains of "Oh beautiful for spacious skies" spread across the encampment, the prisoners seemed to stand a little straighter, a little stronger, with a glimmer of hope on their faces. They sang "The Star-Spangled Banner" and "God Bless America," and during the service, the Japanese honor guard, ordered there by Captain Konno, stood at rigid attention in honor of the deceased President.

Taylor walked to the center of the men and said, "We didn't know him personally, but we knew his thoughts were of us. He was a man who knew pain, a man of tenderness, yet of great courage. The world will miss him tomorrow as we miss him today."

He then invited the Americans to face the west, in honor of their beloved President, and while the Australian bugler sounded taps, the scraggly prisoners rendered a final salute. To their amazement, the Japanese presented arms during taps.

As each hospital patient regained enough strength

to walk, he was immediately assigned to work in Japan's largest coal mines near Fukuoka 22. For Taylor, his right arm still weak, the fourteen-hour day of picking the glowing carbon from the walls inside the tunnel was a painful exercise. Yet it was a welcome diversion from the hospital routine, and his body soon adjusted to the hard labor. Taylor marveled at how precisely God had made his body so that it would adjust to nearly any new circumstance and fight for life as long as his mind would not give up.

Unsanitary conditions in the mine caused much misery. It was painful for the four tuberculosis patients to breathe the coal dust, but the guards, against the continual protest of the Australian medical officers, forced any man who could move to walk the several miles to and from the mines, and any man who reported late for the long march was severely beaten.

Once each month the guards issued one razor blade to each prisoner and Taylor was sure more than one had given considerable thought to slitting a Japanese throat with the blades, though none ever tried it.

By the end of the month the blade was so dull it pulled the whiskers out by the roots. Taylor would fastidiously strop it against the heel of his hand, although it actually honed it very little.

Taylor had his first experienced with washing clothes in winter, and he discovered it took considerable nerve to plunge his scaly, red hands into the icy water. But clean clothes were such a rarity, he never hesitated.

The food ration for each man who worked in the mines was supposed to be about seven hundred grams of rice per day, but Taylor knew it was far less. Occasionally, a small portion of fish and a few vegetables were included.

On the way to and from work, Taylor saw many Japanese peasants who quite obviously were suffering from lack of food. If their own people are needful, Taylor thought, what can a POW expect?

Taylor gazed in awe at the tall, brown smokestacks above the crematoriums, and learned from Captain Konno that it was impossible to bury all the Japanese dead in cemeteries as was done in America. There were too many people and too little space.

When men in Fukuoka 22 died, their bodies mysteriously disappeared, with no explanation from the Japanese. Taylor had a strange feeling he knew where the bodies were being taken.

As the work crew passed through the little hamlets, they saw kimono-clad women and old men in high wooden shoes going to and from the hot baths. Scraggly horses pulled wooden carts through the dusty streets.

From time to time Taylor gathered weeds and boiled them in a tin can. He didn't know how much nourishment would be derived, but it relieved the hunger pangs slightly.

South Japan was bitter cold during those early weeks of 1945. There were no fires anywhere in the camp, and often the prisoners shoveled snow from the roofs to keep them from collapsing. The only time Taylor was warm was night when he was heavily covered by blankets.

Each Sunday morning he conducted worship services, and the response of the American and Australian prisoners greatly encouraged him. The Communion services were particularly meaningful. Services were also held for the men still in the hospital and once each month Communion was given to them.

Then one day there was great excitement in Fukuoka 22. The prisoners sighted long-range American bombers over Hakata Bay. Most of the ensuing raids were carried out at night, and although the Japanese had provided air-raid shelters for the prisoners, there was always the fear of again being bombed by their own planes. For weeks, during the air attacks just before dawn, the prisoners raced for the damp, cold sub-surface shelter.

"Bloody awful to get zapped by the Allies," Captain Moore remarked one time as he entered the shelter.

"Yeah," Taylor replied.

Another Australian officer named James Chichester crawled over beside Taylor and said, "Nasty, I'll tell you, nasty."

Taylor nodded assent.

"Wretched blokes anyway," he said. "Holding those packages."

"What packages?" Taylor asked.

"You haven't heard, Yank? Red Cross packages arrived in old Fukuoka 22 yesterday."

"Why weren't they distributed?"

"When we saw them being placed in the old storehouse, we went to the commandant and protested, but got no relief," Captain Moore replied.

"That's right," the other officer added. "The bloody Nip captain told us the parcels were being placed in storage for imminent emergency."

"Which means the Nip is siphoning it off for himself and his dingy little beach climbers, that's the truth of it," Captain Moore said.

As far as Taylor knew, the parcels never reached the prisoners.

The siren sounded the all clear and the prisoners returned to their barracks for an hour's sleep before reporting for the daily trek to the coal mines.

As Taylor pulled the heavy blankets over him, he soon discovered his mind was too active for sleep. He thought mainly of his fellow prisoners and their display of living Christian faith and optimism. Instead of becoming bitter and blasphemous, they were humble and unselfish, always thinking of the other men. Except for that time when their morale seemed to be completely broken under the duress of enclosure in the hell ships, they shared their Christian experience during times of devotion and sang lustily. The power faith brought was amazing.

That night, Captain Konno, once again called Taylor to his quarters.

"Komban wa, Chaplain Taylor," he said as Taylor stepped up onto the tatami mat.

"Good evening, Captain."

"Tomorrow you leave Fukuoka."

"Oh?"

"You are being transferred."

Taylor was silent.

"You have been happy here, Chaplain Taylor?"

Again Taylor did not reply.

"We have been told that what we do is for our emperor. Do you believe that, Chaplain Taylor?"

"We do what we do."

"As school children we are taught:

"Let Mikado's empire stand

"Till a thousand years, ten thousand years roll on,

"Till the sand in the brooklets grow to stone,

"And the moss these emeralds make.

"That, Chaplain Taylor, is from Japanese National Anthem."

"It's very beautiful."

This night the captain was drinking sake instead of Japanese green tea. He poured it from a long, green bottle with a narrow neck and a small rope saddle for carrying Then it was heated to a certain temperature before serving. He offered some to Taylor.

"Could I have the tea?" Taylor asked.

The officer clapped his hand, and an aide rushed in with the tea.

"We are doomed, Chaplain Taylor. It's finished. We have lost."

Taylor sipped the green tea and munched a rice cracker.

"As a Japanese schoolboy is punished for violation of unwritten codes of behavior, morality and custom, so we are exposed to the ridicule and even exile from the family of nations."

The more sake he drank, the more he talked.

"The strict stratification of Japanese life majors on the insignificance of the individual, Chaplain Taylor,' he continued, pouring himself another cup of sake. "Thus the Japanese is trained to adjust to a prescribed way of life in an authoritarian atmosphere."

"But you seem to have broken out of the prescribed way."

"Tonight, maybe – tomorrow, no. We never break out. Vary a degree to the left, a degree to the right, but never break out."

Taylor thought the captain talked as though the spiritual time vault of his heart had begun to open. He apparently found no consolation in the tragic ruins of his human idol.

"A man survives on the basis of his decisions, Captain," he said. "A decision is a split second in eternity –

right or wrong. And to be right is a heavenly gift when robed in humility. Take Jesus Christ, for instance."

"What about him?"

"He was robed in humility. And Gandhi said if Christians were like Christ, he would become one. His life was a document of truth."

"Gandhi?"

"Christ."

"Remove the scales of humanity, and all men are the same."

"No, Captain, men are different."

"We Christians?"

Taylor wondered.

"If Japan had won the war, we would have placed symbols of our religion – Shinto shrines and Buddhist temples – on every mountain in America. From everywhere you would have seen these symbols. But what will you Christians do for my country?"

Taylor pondered the question, then answered, "Captain, I have a gift for you. It is a New Testament. I would invite you to read it."

"We Japanese have erected a wall where faith begins. Someone must unlock the door to the world we are hiding in. Maybe Jesus Christ. I hope so."

"I hope so, too," Taylor replied.

"Had our armies won, we immediately would have sent priests and monks to educate the American people in our religion. It was on the drawing board of the master plan."

He paused, and then continued, "Had our troopships reached your ports, the first men down the gangplank would have been our religious men. I hope you will send your religious men to help lift us from the destruction of war."

"Perhaps we will. I pray we will," Taylor replied.

The next morning the bugler, who had been nick-named Harry James, blew reveille, and the Japanese guards rushed into each barrack and ordered the prisoners to assemble in the yard. A fleet of Nissan trucks pulled into Fukuoka 22, and the POWs were told they had ten minutes to eat and gather their clothes.

Minutes later, Taylor was scanning the desolate, almost barren Japanese countryside from the back of a truck, as the convoy moved toward Hakata Bay. Farmers labored meticulously, trying to cultivate their rice crops. He hoped their labors were not in vain. People along the roadside seemed unhappy and discouraged. Apparently the bitter effects of war already had reached the Japanese mainland.

At noon the convoy pulled into Fukuoka City and proceeded to the port, where they parked near a long pier. Taylor cringed at the thought of another sea voyage. But eight hour later, when the guards ordered the POWs from the beach up the gangplank of the ship, Taylor was surprised that they were not forced into the holds. Instead, soldiers carrying machine guns ordered the prisoners into the comfortable quarters below. Each man received a life vest and was promised food.

At 4 o'clock the next morning, when the vessel weighed anchor, the interpreter told them that their destination was Korea and they were to land at 5 p.m.

When Taylor spotted Father Duffey, he thought it was too good to be true, and actually pinched himself to see if he were dreaming. He was not. Duffey had been interned in another work camp near Saga, and now there was a joyful reunion. Together they ate healthy portions of fish and rice that were served.

Several American officers in the group had been unable to walk when they left Fukuoka 22, and the ship's doctor attended them. Nevertheless, at 2 p.m., Major Smothers, one of the patients, died. Taylor requested and received permission to conduct a religious ceremony, while a detail wrapped the body in a white sheet and prepared it for burial.

Taylor opened his Bible and read, "For God so loved the world that he gave his only begotten Son; that whosoever believeth in him should not perish, but have everlasting life. We believe this beautiful promise. The body returns to dust, but no man can destroy the immortal soul. It belongs only to God.

Then Taylor prayed, and as the detail lifted the white bundle over the side of the ship, the Japanese officers present joined the Americans and Australians in a salute to the dead.

Major Smothers was the last of more than eleven hundred deaths Taylor witnessed after leaving the Philippines, the last of more than seven hundred funerals. The chaplain remembered him as devout man who never missed a devotional service. Before he had died, he called Taylor to his bedside to tell him," I don't mind passing on so much, Chaplain, it's just my wife and my little girl. Who will take care of them now?"

"The same God who stood by you these many months surely will stand by them," Taylor answered.

14.

MANCHURIA

At 5 o'clock that evening, the ship sailed into Pusan Harbor, at the head of the Naktong River Basin in Korea. The prisoners disembarked and marched into the city. Taylor was captivated by the beauty of Pusan, where small houses were set in the sides of the mountains that surrounded the city.

After marching through the business district, the prisoners were herded into the city's main auditorium, where Korean laborers had removed the seats and had placed mats on the floor for the prisoners. Soon they brought rice and fish. Morale was high. Not only had they experienced a safe voyage, now they were warn and comfortable.

Before long, the Japanese senior officer appeared with his interpreter to inform the prisoners that he hoped to make their stay comfortable until they went on to Manchuria.

"Manchuria!" Captain Moore echoed. "Who's the bloody rats going to Manchuria?"

The officer continued his speech above the whispers of the surprised prisoners.

Reveille sounded at 6 a.m. and the guards led the men, in columns of two, out of the auditorium and toward the railroad station, where a first-class passenger train was standing on the tracks. Within a few minutes the train was loaded and began moving north up the peninsula to Manchuria.

Taylor watched the passing countryside with great interest. He had never been there before, but he had heard of the legendary beauty of the mountain ranges along the eastern coast.

"Korea very nice," the interpreter said, as he approached the seat where Taylor and the priest were sitting.

"Yes, very nice," Duffey said.

"Japanese influence very strong here."

"Yes it is," Taylor replied, thinking of the misery the peasants must have endured under the iron fist of Tokyo.

Taylor had heard that most Koreans were Buddhists and Confucianists, with a native mixture, called Chon-do-gyo, that endorsed certain teachings from all the world's great religions, including Christianity, and fused them into one. He wondered how it all worked.

Food was well prepared and abundant. The prisoners could look forward to three rations per day. In one instance, the Japanese doctor on board refused to let the prisoners eat breakfast, which he felt was unsanitary, and immediately had it replaced with another meal.

The train traveled day and night, stopping only for fuel and rations, until early one morning the interpreter stepped into the car to announce they were about to cross the Yalu River into Manchuria.

Every man on the train strained his eye to catch the first glimpse of the fabled waterway, natural boundary between Korea and Manchuria. Taylor pressed his face against the window of the train and saw shallow-draft vessels floating downstream in the muddy waters of the Yalu. He also saw several other bridge spans crossing the river.

The Manchurian countryside was very little different from Korea. Wide-eyes peasants stared at the train as it rumbled past to arrive two hours later in Mukden where they detrained and marched across the city to the Hoten prison camp.

Taylor stepped inside his assigned barracks, and for the first time since he was transferred from the tropics to the cold of Japan, he saw heating facilities; huge coal stoves.

He learned that some of the prisoners had been in Hoten for several years. About two thousand arrived right after the fall of the Philippines in 1942. During the first winter, two hundred died of exposure. Then conditions improved and the early arrivals were treated much better, and except for boredom, things hadn't been so bad.

Compared to the prisoners from Fukuoka 22, the men looked strong and healthy. But the new prisoners were separated from the other men and kept in isolation, even though the rules were not rigidly observed and the old Hoten hands visited the new arrivals each night.

When they saw the emaciated bodies, they did everything they could to help. Most of the new men weighed less than a hundred pounds, so the old-timers gathered as much food as possible and brought it to them. Some of the men worked in Japanese factories in Mukden and each day brought fresh supplies from the city.

One evening a tall, dark man approached Taylor and introduced himself as Captain Bates. When Taylor asked how the captain knew he was a chaplain, Bates explained that he had attended Taylor's services on Bataan under Colonel Doane.

Captain Bates introduced Taylor to the camp, showing him the mess hall, laundry room, latrines, and the little chapel the men had constructed at the north end of the walled enclosure. Later in the evening, the senior chaplain, Major O'Brien, came to the barracks to call on Taylor and Duffey and invited them to share the worship services with him and the two Australian chaplains who were already in the camp.

"You have things organized real well," Father Duffey told him.

"Not really, Chaplain. I've carried the load here and haven't done too good a job – not like you boys in Cabanatuan."

"Oh, you know about Cabanatuan" Taylor asked.

Word reached every prison camp in the Orient that God was alive in Cabanatuan. It encouraged us all."

"Well, what do you know about that?" Father Duffey said.

At Hoten they had regular worship on Sundays and midweek Bible studies, as well as a lot of counseling, and Taylor returned to the ministry with enthusiasm and vigor. He soon learned that prisoners who are bored have their own set of problems, mainly emotional, from having so little to do. The religious services helped some, but most of the men just wanted to talk to someone, and Preston Taylor was a good listener.

Only weeks after the new prisoners arrived at Hoten, a squadron of American B-29s approached Mukden and destroyed several munitions factories. However, two of the bombs missed their targets and exploded inside Hoten. Seventeen POWs died, and one hundred more were wounded.

Dr. Sadaharu Wadda, the camp doctor, ordered the Japanese guards to carry all the wounded prisoners into the camp hospital and worked without sleep for three days and nights treating them. He saved more than a dozen lives and endeared himself to the hearts of the prisoners. The camp commander, Colonel, also showed great interest in the wounded men and visited the hospital daily.

Slowly but steadily the health of the new arrivals improved. They were released from "isolation" and placed in the barracks with the other prisoners. Dr. Wadda continued to minister to the bed patients.

Taylor had several discussions with the doctor and learned he had been a professor at the Imperial University Hospital in Sapporo, Hokkaido before the war. He had little sympathy for the war or for the Japanese military, and he did not try to hide his feelings, even from the Japanese commander.

Taylor guessed that the doctor's influence caused the prisoners to be treated as soldier and not as dog, and camp scuttlebutt said Dr. Wadda once slapped a Japanese officer who was beating a prisoner.

Taylor often visited the doctor's quarters in early evening, except when there was some kind of hospital emergency. One evening there was none.

"Welcome, Chaplain Taylor. You would join me in Japanese green tea?

"Yes, Doctor, please."

The doctor drank the tea with loud slurping noises and inhaled deeply after each swallow.

"Eee, to, ne," he would say before speaking in English. "What do you think of Manchuria, Chaplain Taylor?"

"It is very cold, but the warm buildings make it comfortable."

"What do you think of Japanese soldiers?"

Taylor pondered the question for several minutes. The doctor continued to slurp the green tea and munch on sembei rich crackers.

"I don't understand Japanese people," Taylor finally replied.

"You no understand Japanese psychology. Neither do Japanese psychologists understand Japanese psychology." Dr. Wadda laughed.

"How do you mean?"

"Japanese men are bad in the head," he said, patting the top of his head. "All mixed up."

"Could you explain? I would be interested in understanding better."

"It starts when little boy. He can do anything – pinch his mother, hit his sister – his father only laughs. But let him get six years old and he goes to school. Then if he does not act right, he disgrace family. They put thumb on his and make him conform."

"And what does that do?"

"It causes great emotional problem. He grows up in conformity after six years of no conformity. Very bad."

"So in times of stress he must find an outlet," Taylor suggested.

"Yes, and does so by brutality. Many times I tell Japanese high command in Tokyo, but they laugh and say Japanese soldier tough. But man need not be tough to butcher women and children, throw babies into air and catch on bayonets, and run bayonets through women's breasts. That crazy."

All of Taylor's questions weren't answered, but he understood the Japanese mind better. For the first time he fully realized how much effect culture has on people and their attitudes.

Taylor made many calls on the doctor. Together they discussed Japanese customs, history, military might, and even Christianity, although the doctor showed only a superficial interest in the latter. Nevertheless, Taylor prayed for him every day.

A new phenomenon arose in camp – liberation fever. The prisoners were confident it wouldn't be long in coming, since the Chinese who worked alongside the prisoners in the factories passed on bits of news and gossip, and the prisoners brought the rumors back to camp.

During July and august the rumors increased, and some prisoners put such stock in them that they actually packed their few belongings and prepared to leave.

Chinese newspapers smuggled into camp told of a massive fire-bombing raid over Tokyo and the threat of a Soviet invasion from Siberia, and even the Japanese guards talked freely to the prisoners of the possibility that the war might end.

Then it happened. At 11 a.m. on August 15, 1945, the prisoners saw a large plane circling the outskirts of the city of Mukden. As it flew over Hoten, six men bailed out over the camp, their parachutes carrying them close to the enclosure.

"They're blasted Russian parachute troops," Captain Moore told Taylor.

"No. That's no Soviet plane. That's American," Taylor shouted.

The men were delirious with excitement. They jumped up and down and danced around jubilantly. The Japanese guards withdrew their rifles and removed their swords. Then a roar rattled the prison walls as the huge wooden gates sprung open and the six Americans marched into Hotel prison to be greeted exuberantly by the POWs.

A detail was assigned to stay near the headquarters to keep an eye on the surrender negotiations, and the first report was that the six Americans were sitting around a table drinking Japanese green tea with the commandant, Colonel it.

There was another round of celebration, and the men yelled until their throats were hoarse.

Taylor stepped to the rear of the throng of men and looked up into the dark Manchurian sky.

"Dear God, there were times I didn't know about it all, other times I didn't think I would make it. Your goodness saw me through. I'll never understand why the others – Morris, Bill, and all the others – didn't make it. But tonight I want to rededicate my life to re-building this burned-out world, and build it on peace and love and brotherhood. Hear this prayer I make in Jesus' name. Amen."

No one slept during the night. The halls of the barracks were jammed with shouting men who had reached the end of prison life. Taylor spent most of the evening thinking of his wife Ione and found it difficult to believe that he would soon be seeing her again.

Heretofore, Japanese guards had paraded through the barracks every hour on the hour during the night. This night, none came. On previous nights all lights were extinguished at 9 p.m. This night the lights stayed on all night.

The next morning a voice over the loudspeaker asked all the men to assemble in the prison yard, and there, on a raised platform in the center of the compound, Colonel Ito formally surrender his sword to General Parker, asking the general to take over the internal affairs of the camp, while he volunteered Japanese patrols to form a perimeter guard to protect the camp from outside violence. The gesture seemed very strange to Taylor, but he later heard of raging battles in downtown Mukden between the Japanese and Chinese. Meanwhile, General Parker stepped to the microphone to tell the prisoner that they were free men, that America had won the war, and that the Japanese had surrendered and all prison camps were now being liberated.

The general paused until the thunderous applause subsided, then added: "Our fly boys will be dropping food and supplies this evening."

Well-dressed, well-groomed and smiling, the six Americans looked like giants compared to the prisoners.

Hour after hour the prisoners talked to them and listened to details of the atom-bomb drops on Hiroshima and Nagasaki.

"Atom bomb?" one of the men asked.

The former prisoners asked more questions than the six could answer in a month, but they talked till late in the night. General Parker told the men they would all be evacuated from Manchuria in a few days. He also announced that a Russian army had occupied Mukden and would visit Hoten later.

"Meanwhile, enjoy the food."

And they did. Too much. Several became ill on the first full stomach in three and one-half years, so that Dr. Wadda had to set up an eating program calculated to gradually restore their eating capacity.

That night, General parker summoned the seventeen hundred Americans and Australians to assemble near the headquarters building.

"Our allies have arrived," he said. "Since they're to occupy Manchuria, they have formally come to liberate us."

As the men laughed, the gates swung open and a small group of Russians in high black boots marched stiffly into camp.

A Russian propaganda officer stood on the steps of the headquarters building and addressed the men through an interpreter. He was very generous in his remarks and congratulatory to the other allies, then finished: "It is indeed a pleasure for the Red army to have the privilege of liberating the prisoners of war." The men cheered him for several minutes, to his great delight, and his broad face beamed.

The Russian major also announced that earlier in the day Emperor Hirohito of Japan had broken five years of silence and broadcast a speech to the Japanese people over the radio. The major then read the text of the Emperor's message: "We have resolved to pave the way for a grand peace for all generations to come by enduring the unendurable and suffering what is insufferable."

Then the Russian major ordered the Japanese to march out of the camp to surrender their weapons formally, but as the Japanese formed two columns and prepared to leave, a voice called to General Parker, "What about Dr. Wadda? We still need him in the hospital." The general requested, and received, permission from the propaganda officer to keep the doctor in the hospital.

Within a few hours after the formal liberation, the chaplains conducted a service of thanksgiving, and Taylor believed that every person in the camp – except the patients in the hospital – attended.

As Taylor stood to speak, the great host of liberated

men fell silent.

"For three and one-half years we've prayed for liberation. Now our prayers are answered. To God be the glory! Not only are we happy, but we are humbled, and in that humility must commit ourselves to rebuilding a world where such a war can never occur again. We're going back to our families soon. Let's go back with the Love of God in our hearts and his word in our hands. Let's tell the world what God did in Cabanatuan, Bilibid, O'Donnell, Fukuoka 22 and Hoten. This is not the end but the beginning. Let's turn the world right side up – for God and four our country."

Then he stepped down, and Father Duffey closed the service by leading the Lord's Prayer. As the men prayed, Taylor looked at them – the hardened combat troops – and saw no dry eye among them.

Just after the close of the service, a lookout in the tower spotted a flight of B-29s, and soon the sky was white with parachutes dropping supplies to Hoten. The food, clothing and much-needed medicine were quickly carried into camp and distributed.

The Russians were very cordial, issuing passes to the city of Mukden, taking some of the prisoners on airplane rides round the city, and showing great kindness to all the hospitalized. They also announced that General Wainwright had been liberated from another camp in Mukden and at that moment was on his way to Japan to meet General MacArthur.

This was confirmed the next evening by a radio broadcast from Free China: "He was haggard and aged. He struggled to walk with the help of a cane. His eyes were sunken and cheeks pitted, his hair snow white. But he made a brave effort to smile as MacArthur embraced him."

The newscaster continued: "This, observers say, was the most moving account yet to come out of the war in the Pacific.

"For three years Wainwright imagined himself a disgrace for having surrendered Corregidor. A shocked General MacArthur declared him one of the great heroes of our time and recommended him for the Medal of Honor. He also offered Wainwright his old command.

Taylor was gathering together his few belongings – a Bible, a letter from his mother, and a few mementos from Hoten – when Father Duffey walked into the barracks. Sadly, he told Taylor he was going to China with the hospital patients.

It had been a long way from Bataan. The only two surviving chaplains from the hell ships said their final good-by with fierce hugs and tearful eyes.

15.

AND HOME

On September 11, Russian Trucks moved into Hoten and picked up the remaining POWs, including Taylor. The nightmare had ended.

First-class passenger trains were standing by at the railroad station to transfer the men to Dairen on the Yellow Sea, and when they reached the port, Taylor knew it was one of his life's greatest moments when he saw against the black China night, the illuminated Red Cross on the hospital ship U.S.S. Relief. The men were graciously received by the doctors and nurses on the ship, and those who needed medical attention were cared for promptly.

The ship weighed anchor that night and sailed for Okinawa, arriving there on September 15. Once again Taylor was wrapped in nostalgia as the Navy band played "Anchors Aweigh," "Wild Blue Yonder," and "The Caissons Go Rolling Along." But war is not like that, he thought. It's so different. So very different.

Upon arrival in Okinawa the men received new uniforms. Then they were alerted for a flight back to Manila, a 900-mile trip that took only a few hours, quite a contrast to Taylor's last crossing on the prison ships.

When they arrived in the Philippines, the men were given thorough medical examinations and each man received a one-grade promotion in rank.

Though Taylor had never thought about it before, "Major Taylor" sounded mighty good.

A number of the men received medals, many the Purple Heart, the badge of military merit created by George Washington in 1782 for those wounded in action. Although Taylor had been wounded twice he did not receive the medal, since both times he had been injured by bombs from American planes and not the enemy.

Taylor knew it would be painful, but he had to visit Cabanatuan. The train ride from Manila took only a few hours, and an army jeep was waiting to take him out to the prison, already virtually deserted. A few carabao were grazing inside, and a couple of Filipino MPs stared nonchalantly at him as he stopped in front of the main gate.

He got out of the jeep and walked toward the camp cemetery. It was a quiet and reverent place, already reconditioned by the American army. The grass had been cut and a fence erected to keep the water buffalo away. New markers had been placed where bamboo crosses once stood. Americans always take good care of their dead, Taylor thought.

As the compound gate he smiled at the guards, who stood to attention, saluting briskly. He walked slowly inside and stared at the deserted rows of buildings. Weeds had grown up around the parade ground; the solitary cells had been torn down; an American flag waved in the Philippine wind.

Then he returned to Manila, and, after the completion of processing in the replacement depot, sailed for the States on the U. S. S Marine Shark. He spent most of the twenty-three days on the ship eating, sleeping and talking to the men he hadn't seen since Bataan and Cabanatuan, and chafing impatiently to see Ione. He hoped she had received his telegram from Manila.

On November 2, the ship sailed into San Francisco Bay and under the Golden Gate Bridge. He was home.

Ione had received the telegram and met him at the dock. As he walked down the gangplank she stared at him, her long, black hair blowing in the wind.

He threw his arms around her but she did not respond. Rather, she drew back and stood away from him.

"Preston, I've done a terrible thing."

He looked at her in silence.

"I'm remarried."

For several minutes Taylor stared silently out over the harbor, oblivious to the joyous bedlam around them. After a while, Ione said, "My car is waiting," and she led him through the throngs of people to the parked car. They drove across town to a restaurant, and he took her hand as she slipped through the door.

How little she has changed, he thought, looking at her angular nose and beautiful pale skin. The string of pearls he had sent her from Manila beautifully accented her blue dress. But she was not wearing the ring he had given her during the wedding ceremony in Fort Worth. It had been replaced by a solid gold band.

"You look well, Preston – as well as could be expected, I guess."

"You're as beautiful as ever, Ione."

Then neither spoke for a long while. They sipped their water, fidgeted with their silverware, shifted back and forth in their chairs until finally he asked, "What happened, Ione?"

She moistened her dry lips and swallowed before speaking.

"For nearly four years I waited and had faith you

would return. I saw, heard, smelled, and almost tasted the past."

She paused, sipped again at her water.

"Go on."

"Well, last year I met this man and we dated some. Then he asked me to marry him but I refused."

Yes?"

"Then in January, Colonel Oliver and several of your friends were freed from Cabanatuan. They came through San Francisco, and ..." She broke into tears, sobbing softly as she tried to continue.

"They told me you had died on the ships to Japan, and when I heard it I remarried, just last month."

The tear slid down her cheeks and onto the linen tablecloth.

"It's too late for us."

"But why, Ione? I still love you. I don't care if you have remarried. I still love you and need you."

"Preston, try to understand. I haven't seen you in four years, and I'm already living with another man. Can't you see? We're no longer married."

He looked at the sobbing Ione across the table and a thousand memories flashed through his mind. He felt so alone. For a moment he wondered if God had forsaken him, too. But then the doubt passed. He knew God had been by his side along. He was there now.

"You're still a great gal, Ione. It's okay." He got up, squeezed her hand gently and walked out into the misty San Francisco morning.

Epilogue

Following his return to the United States, Major Robert Preston Taylor was given one hundred and five days' convalescent leave. After spending several days under observation in San Francisco, he was transferred to a military hospital in Temple, Texas where he was united with his family.

During those days he faced a great decision – whether or not to remain a minister in uniform. He thought seriously of returning to the pastorate, but each time he did so a deep sadness gripped him. Then he settled it – he would remain in the chaplaincy.

In January of 1946, Taylor was appointed Chaplain, Headquarters, Army Air Forces Training Command, Barksdale Field, Louisiana.

He later served as Wing Chaplain, Mather Air Force Base, California; Deputy Staff Chaplain, Air Materiel Command, Wright-Patterson Air Force Base, Ohio; Chaplain for Civil Air Patrol Headquarters, Washington, D.C.; and Staff Chaplain of the Air University, Maxwell Air Force Base, Alabama.

During those years he pieced together bits of information about his many friends from Cabanatuan.

Father Duffey returned to a parish in Canton, Ohio, and Taylor saw him many times.

Morris Day had been executed by the Japanese on another ship bound from Mindanao to Japan.

Colonel Oliver, chief of chaplains in the Philippines,

returned to the Midwest.

Doctors North and Schwartz returned to private practice.

Colonel Harold K. Johnson, one of the commandants in Cabanatuan, later became chief of staff of the United States Army.

Marvin Denny, his jeep driver, entered the ministry.

In 1958, President Dwight D. Eisenhower named Taylor Deputy Chief of Air Force Chaplains, Headquarters, United States Air Force, with the rank of Brigadier General.

Four years later, upon recommendation of General Curtis LeMay, President John F. Kennedy named him Air Force Chief of Chaplains, with the rank of Major General.

A number of personal friends and Air Force officials attended the Pentagon ceremony and saw his wife, Millie, the former Millie Good, whom he had married several years earlier, pin the Major General stars on her husband's shoulders.

Later, upon inquiry concerning his personal thoughts during the ceremony, he characteristically replied, "I just wanted to get it over with so I could get on with my job of helping all those men in uniform to whom I felt a strong sense of commitment."

Bill Keith is an award-winning journalist who served as an investigative reporter, city editor and editor of three newspapers in Louisiana and Texas. He was a war correspondent in Vietnam and also had assignments in Tokyo, the Philippines and West Berlin and traveled in 35 other countries.

He earned the bachelor of arts in journalism from Wheaton College in Illinois, the master of divinity from the Southwestern Baptist Theological Seminary in Fort Worth, Texas, and a graduate diploma from the Tokyo School of the Japanese Language.

Through the years he served as the director of public relations for the Baptist General Convention of Texas in Dallas; a Louisiana state senator representing the people of Shreveport, Louisiana; senior editor of Huntington House Books, Inc.; and president and chief fundraiser for the Academic Freedom Legal Defense Fund.

His written works include Days of Anguish, Days of Hope (Doubleday); W. A. Criswell, the Authorized Biography (Fleming Revell); The Commissioner (Pelican Publishing Co.); Scopes II/the Great Debate and The Divine Connection (Huntington House, Inc.); Joy Comes in the Morning (Fellowship Foundation); and others.

He and his wife Vivian Marie live in Longview, Texas, where he works as a full-time writer of both fiction and non-fiction books. His email address is Bigscribe@aol.com and his website is located at:
www.BillKeithBooks.com.
His mailing address is P. O. Box 8321, Longview, TX 75607.

OTHER BOOKS BY BILL KEITH

The Commissioner is the intriguing true story of death and deception and reveals a corrupt political battle during the 1970s that threatened Shreveport, Louisiana. The city's police commissioner -- the most powerful lawman in the state -- was behind multiple scandals including racism, payoffs, theft of city funds and tampering with a grand jury. He may also have been involved in the murder of an advertising executive who was scheduled to testify against him in court. (Available at your local book store)

The Prayer Bag and Other Stories that Warm the Heart takes the reader on a spiritual journey through the prayer lives of some of the greatest Christians the world has ever known... a missionary in the jungles of Sumatra who prayed for a nail and found one; a survivor of the dread Ravensbruck Concentration Camp in Germany who prayed for a brutal guard who brutalized her sister while in the camp; an evangelist who witnessed to Emperor Hirohito of Japan after World War II; and a preacher who carried a cross around the world. "And you will read about my dear wife Vivian Marie who carries a prayer bag with her everywhere she goes." ~ The Author (Available through Stonegate Publishing Co. Inc. at Stonegatebooks@aol.com)

Joy Comes in the Morning is the true story of one of the greatest miracles of the Twentieth Century. Delores Winder, a Presbyterian lady, was an invalid for 19 years and was planning her funeral when God intervened in her life. She was completely healed during a United

Methodist Church Conference on the Holy Spirit in Dallas, Texas, in 1975. Since that time she and her husband Bill have traveled throughout the world telling her amazing story. (Available at www.BillKeithBooks.com)

The Magic Bullet is a novel about a scientist who discovers the secret of life extension. However, the discovery creates all kinds of problems for him. A recluse billionaire in Chicago -- who is dying -- wants to find the secret and sends his men to kidnap the scientist. Also, the Chinese government hires a New York City Mafia don to find the scientist and learn the secret. The scientist hides out in the Barataria swamps below New Orleans and joins a motorcycle gang en route to the biker's rally at Sturgis, South Dakota, where he is captured by the billionaire's men and taken to Chicago. The reader will laugh and cry but will never forget the dramatic climax. (Available through StoneGate Publishing Co. at Stonegatebooks@aol.com.)

Gettin' Old Ain't for Sissies is a motivational and inspirational book to help the baby boomers and older survive and enjoy the senior years. The thesis is: "Old age doesn't have to be the end of the line. It can be a bright new beginning." The book outlines the five things a person must do to live a vigorous lifestyle into the 70s, 80s and even the 90s and gives numerous examples of Older Champions. (Available through StoneGate.)

Look for these books in the future: *The Guns of Winter* (A novel about one man's war with Washington); W. A. Criswell/the Authorized Biography about the dynamic pastor of the First Baptist Church of Dallas, Texas, and a man believed by some to be the greatest preacher of the Twentieth Century; Days of Rage about the Tulsa, Oklahoma, race riot of 1921 where white vigilantes killed some 300 black people and burned some 1200 homes and businesses.

CPSIA information can be obtained
at www.ICGtesting.com
Printed in the USA
LVOW12s0055280717
542940LV00001B/29/P